Reading *for First*

with Answer key

Series editors:

Malcolm Mann • Steve Taylore-Knowles

MACMILLAN

Macmillan Education
4 Crinan Street
London N1 9XW
A division of Macmillan Publishers Limited

Companies and representatives throughout the world

ISBN 978-0-230-46095-9 (with key)
ISBN 978-0-230-46098-0 (without key)
ISBN 978-0-230-46093-5 (with key + MPO Pack)
ISBN 978-0-230-46092-8 (without key + MPO Pack)

Designed by emc design ltd
Cover photograph courtesy of Getty Images/YouraPechkin
Picture research by Emily Taylor

Malcolm Mann and Steve Taylore-Knowles would like to thank
everyone at Macmillan and signature manuscripts for their hard
work on this challenging but greatly enjoyable project.

The publishers would like to thank all those who participated
in the development of this project, with special thanks to the
freelance editor.

The authors and publishers would like to thank the following for
permission to reproduce their material:
Alamy/All Canada Photos p47, Alamy/Blend Images p25,
Alamy/Ron Buskirk p10, Alamy/ Richard Levine p64, Alamy/
Robert Marmion p65, Alamy/OJO Images p7, Alamy/ Photos 12
p95; **Corbis**/Matt Bird p87, Corbis/Gaetano p96, Corbis/Robbie
Jack p56; **Getty Images**/Age fotostock p33, Getty Images/Don
Bayley p15(br), Getty Images/Annabelle Breakey p43, Getty
Images/Kerstin Klaassen p90, Getty Images/Geri Lavrov p88,
Getty Images/Ryan McVay p34, Getty Images/Stuart O'Sullivan
p31, Getty Images/Art Wolfe p49, Getty Images/James
Woodson p80; **Glow Images**/Aurora Open p8-9, Glow Images/
Brooklyn Production/Corbis p15(tr); **Image Source**/Cultura p17,
Image Source/Moodboard pp42, 73, Image Source/OJO Images
p79; **Plain Picture**/Hamidanoglu Golten p55, Plain Picture/
Johner p39, Plain Picture/Minden Pictures p48, Plain Picture/
PhotoAlto p63; **Rex Features** pp26, 71, Rex Features/Kevin Foy
p24, Rex Features/Monkey Business Images p23.

Printed and bound in Thailand

2018 2017 2016 2015 2014
10 9 8 7 6 5 4 3 2 1

Contents

Introduction

What is *Improve your Skills: Reading for First*?

Reading for First is part of the *Improve your Skills* exam skills series: four preparation books which cover all aspects of the *Cambridge English: First (FCE)* exam. This course aims to develop the key reading skills, and language and exam techniques, for parts 5–7 of the *First Use of English and Reading* paper. The course can be used in conjunction with the other books in the series: *Use of English for First*, *Writing for First* and *Listening and Speaking for First*. It can also be used as a general skills development course, or as preparation for other general English tests.

How do I use *Improve your Skills*?

You can use any of the books in this series either in class or to study on your own. The course will guide you through the activities step by step, so you can use this book with or without a teacher.

If you are studying as part of a class, your teacher will direct you on how to use each activity. Some activities can be treated as discussions, in which case they can be a useful opportunity to share ideas and techniques with other learners.

How is *Improve your Skills: Reading for First* organised?

The course is made up of 12 units, each aimed at developing a particular reading skill (e.g. *scanning*). Every unit is themed around a commonly occurring topic from the *First* exam.

Each unit consists of:

- **Skills development:** explanation, examples and tasks to develop and practise relevant reading skills both for general use and the exam. Each skill is broken down into simple stages with reference to why each skill is important for *First*.
- **Vocabulary:** useful vocabulary for the First exam.
- **Exam focus and practice:** focus on how each skill relates to the exam, followed by authentic *First* style tasks for real exam practice.

There are also *Skills tip* boxes throughout the book containing useful information and ideas on how to approach the exam reading tasks.

How will *Improve your Skills* increase my chances of exam success?

Skills development

The skills sections form a detailed syllabus of core reading skills which are useful both in the exam and in everyday life – reading for specific information and understanding attitude and opinion, for example. People often do these things in their own language without noticing, so it can take some practice to perform these actions in another language. Learning and understanding vocabulary and grammar can take priority in the classroom, and these very important skills can often get ignored.

Language input

Each unit includes useful vocabulary and phrases for the exam. In *Improve your Skills: Reading for First*, you will find a wide range of topic vocabulary and ideas to make sure that you are well prepared when you reach the real exam.

Exam technique

In any exam, it is important to be prepared for the types of tasks you are likely to be given, and to have methods ready to answer any particular question. The *Exam focus* section helps you develop and practise these methods. The *Skills tip* boxes give short, simple advice about different types of questions, as well as study skills and how to effectively use the skills you have learned. The course covers every question type that you will face in the *First* exam.

How is the *First* exam organised and where does reading fit in?

The *First* exam consists of four papers: *Use of English & Reading, Writing, Speaking* and *Listening.* Parts 5–7 of the *Use of English & Reading* paper test your reading skills. The complete paper takes 1 hour and 15 minutes.

What does each task consist of?

The reading tasks (Parts 5–7) make up 20% of your final mark in *First*. There are three passages which have been taken from a range of sources and aim to test your reading ability in a number of ways. Part 5 is a text followed by six multiple choice questions. Part 6 is a gapped text task – six sentences have been removed which you need to replace with one of seven given options. There are two marks for each question in parts 5 and 6. Part 7 consists of four short texts preceded by ten matching questions. Candidates have to find specific information in the texts in order to answer these questions. Each question is worth one mark in Part 7.

The tasks will test a variety of the following key reading skills:

- Understanding detail and finding specific details
- Understanding gist
- Understanding attitude, opinion and purpose
- Deducing meaning from context and implication
- Identifying main ideas and examples

This course will develop your knowledge and understanding of all of the above skills, as well as the techniques you will need to use when reading, such as scanning and skimming.

Reading for specific information

Team sports

Skill: reading for specific information
Vocabulary: free time topic vocabulary
Exam practice: *First* Paper 1 Part 7

Improve your reading skills: reading for specific information

What is reading for specific information?

*When you read for specific information, you try to find one or more details in a text. These might be names, numbers, times or other types of fact. You know what you are looking for, and you locate the information you need in the text. Sometimes, reading for specific information involves reading to see **if** information is contained in a text.*

1 Which of these is not an example of specific information?

    A a person's name
    B the gist of a text

Why is reading for specific information important?

*Sometimes, you only need part of the information in a long text. For example, a train timetable contains information about many trains and many stations. However, you are probably only interested in one or two trains and one or two stations. Reading for specific information helps you to find **only** the information you need.*

2 You might read something for specific information when you

    A only need some of the information it contains.
    B want to know every piece of information in it.

How do you read for specific information?

First, check for any headings or chapter titles. They may contain the information you need. Then, quickly move your eyes over the words, looking for the place where the specific information appears. This is called 'scanning'. The information might be expressed in different ways, so the ability to predict and paraphrase is important. Once you find the place, read that part carefully, making sure that you understand it.

3 When you scan a text, you

    A try to find a particular piece of information you need.
    B read it quickly to get a general idea of the meaning.

How is reading for specific information important in *First*?

Reading for specific information is particularly important in First *Paper 1 Parts 5 and 7. In Part 5, you need to answer multiple choice questions. This may mean scanning the text and then reading part of the text closely to find information about details, opinions, attitudes, etc. In Part 7, you have to do a matching task. You don't have time to read the whole text slowly and carefully to find the answer to each question, so you need to scan for specific information and then read it carefully.*

4 In *First* Paper 1 Part 7, reading for specific information is useful because it

    A helps you understand every detail of the text.
    B helps you complete the task in time.

Get started

Look at the photo and answer the questions.

- What sporting event does this photo show?
  marathon / relay race / 100 metre sprint
- How much do you think teamwork is a part of this sport?
  very little / none at all / a great deal
- Do you enjoy taking part in or watching this kind of sport? Why / Why not?

Develop your vocabulary

1 Write a word from the box in each gap to complete the phrases.

score ■ defeat ■ lose ■ hold ■ keep

1 _____ the game   4 _____ a record
2 _____ your eye on the ball   5 _____ a goal
3 _____ an opponent

2 Read the paragraph and circle the correct words.

In contrast to individual sports, team sports provide **(1) candidates / participants** with an opportunity to work together to achieve goals. This **(2) friendship / teamwork** teaches players a different set of skills that goes beyond natural **(3) talents / skills** such as being able to run fast or hit the ball hard. Players must make a **(4) group / set** effort to score points and do well in games, especially if they're thinking of winning a competition or national **(5) challenge / championship**. In team sports such as football, basketball and hockey, this means coming up with a winning **(6) strategy / programme** to put into use on the field, court or rink. Obviously, athletes must play in the **(7) titles / positions** to which they're best suited, whether it be striker, midfielder or goalkeeper. There are extra challenges in team sports, such as getting on with your teammates and, for some people, making **(8) tough / rough** decisions for the team. Some team sports involve physical **(9) connection / contact**, making protective clothing such as knee pads and safety **(10) helmets / hats** necessary, as required in cricket and hockey. These concerns aside, team sports are a terrific way for people to achieve common goals, to get some exercise and to make great friends all at once.

Develop your reading skills: reading for specific information

1 Read these excerpts from sports articles and write the competitor's name, sport and accomplishment.

1 With only seconds left in the game, striker Rene Lucci came up from behind to score the winning goal. This will surely make him a name to watch in football.

_____

2 The event, held this year in Sydney, Australia, includes participants from over twenty countries, including the US sailing team led by record holder Alan Lock.

_____

3 The first round of the bowling tournament takes place this Saturday. Don Clark's team, which he helped win last year's top prize, will lead the round.

_____

4 Born in 1895, legendary athlete Babe Ruth is one of the most famous players in American baseball history. In the span of his career, he scored 714 home runs.

_____

5 Other breakthroughs in women's sport include Ann Meyers, who in 1974 became the first high school student to play for a US national team in basketball.

_____

6 We met with Antonio Diez, an Argentine water polo player, to discuss how his team won the gold medal at the men's Water Polo World Championship.

_____

2 Write the numbers of the sentences in exercise 1 that contain the following information. More than one answer may be possible.

1 Important year: _____ **4** Location: _____

2 Day of the week: _____ **5** Name of a competition: _____

3 Reference to a country/nationality: _____ **6** Education level: _____

3 Write a word or phrase from the text in each gap to complete the sentences.

Compared to other team sports, rowing requires a major group effort from athletes. Each rower must move at exactly the same time as every other rower on the team. This can be quite a challenge for large teams that have as many as eight rowers in a single boat. A learner rower will practise with other beginners, along with a trainer, for six to eight weeks in order to learn the necessary skills.

Probably the most important skill is learning how to use the oar, which is the wooden bar that goes into the water. A single rowing stroke involves 'the catch', or putting the oar in the water, and 'the release', or taking it out of the water after pulling. Once this is learned, it's a matter of continual practice as well as muscle training to become a professional athlete.

1 Rowing as a sport involves a big _____ from participants.

2 In rowing, athletes move at _____ as their team-mates.

3 A single team of rowers can consist of as many as _____ rowers.

4 To learn the basic skills, you need from _____ weeks of training.

5 Rowers use a _____ oar to pull the boat.

6 Placing the oar in the water is known as _____.

7 When the oar is taken out of the water, this is called _____.

8 To be an athletic rower, you must combine practice with _____.

4 Match the phrases with the headlines.

1   the beginning of a practice ___
2   a professional gain ___
3   location of a major event ___
4   a type of injury ___
5   details of an exciting game ___
6   a below-standard performance ___

a Football coach **fired** over disappointing loss

b *Draw forces hockey game into thrilling overtime*

c Wembley Stadium to host national championship game

d *Relay runner suffers broken ankle during race*

e Lyle Taylor wins **big** in move from Liverpool to Chelsea

f Training for Olympic rowing team to start Saturday

5 Underline one or two words from the headlines that gave you the answers.

6 Match each article with a headline from exercise 4.

1 ___

Team Green had a great start, scoring one goal in the first ten minutes of the game. The Falcons didn't score their first goal until the game was halfway through. Then, in a dramatic change of luck, their star striker, John Aimes, took control of the match and scored two more goals in less than twenty minutes. When Team Green's coach, Tom Broward, switched goalkeepers towards the end, it was clear that he was desperate to keep the Falcons from scoring again. His plan didn't work. The Falcons went on to score two more goals, winning the game 5-1, and coach Broward was soon out of a job.

2 ___

It was a tragic moment for Ray Stephens, during a competition he and his team must have spent months practising for. Luckily, a medical team arrived on the scene within minutes of the accident. Medics raced onto the track with a stretcher to carry Stephens off to a nearby ambulance. It seems that the accident occurred just as Stephens was passing the baton to fellow runner Neil Lowe. Stephens let go of the baton before Lowe grabbed hold of it. The injury occurred when Stephens jumped forward to keep the baton from hitting the track, falling forward in the process.

7 Read the articles in exercise 6 again and decide if the statements are True (T) or False (F).

1   The Falcons scored their first goal early in the game. ___
2   John Aimes scored the second and third goals for the Falcons. ___
3   Team Green changed players in the last part of the game. ___
4   Ray Stephens waited a long time to receive medical attention. ___
5   Stephens was able to leave the track on his own. ___
6   Lowe was in the process of receiving the baton from Stephens. ___

9

8 Scan the blog posts quickly and complete the chart.

Andy, 21

Practice is going to be tough this year, but I know our team is going to do really well in the competitions this spring. It's difficult waking up at 6am every weekday to be at the court by 7am, especially for practice that lasts an hour and a half, but I really enjoy having a lot of energy throughout the day. My teammates are terrific as well, and we've become great friends. I'm sure we're going to have the best basketball team in the area.

Beth, 22

I meet with my cycling team once a week, but we do our practising on our own. It's definitely a team sport with great emphasis on individual performance. That works really well for me, particularly because I can practise whenever I like. These days, I do it for a couple of hours on Mondays and Wednesdays after my last class which ends at 4pm. It's perfect because I can use the bike trails in the park between school and home. The only drawback is that some team-mates don't meet every week. That's not good for teamwork.

Paul, 22

I'm really excited about this year's polo competition. We've been working really hard every weekend to prepare for it. I'd like to practise more often but, with everyone's busy schedule, it's difficult to meet during the week. But we spend about three hours every Saturday and Sunday on the polo field, and that's enough to get good at it. I have a great time with my horse, too. That's the best thing about it. If only the field were maintained a little better, I'd have no complaints at all.

Player	Andy	Beth	Paul
Sport			
Practice days			
Practice length			
Likes			
Dislikes			

9 Tick the information that is mentioned in the article. Do not read the article from start to finish.

1 the game's origin ___
2 who plays the game ___
3 number of players ___
4 scoring system ___
5 rules of play ___
6 famous players ___
7 penalty rule ___
8 playing area description ___
9 competitions ___
10 where the game is played ___

Perhaps more game than sport, dodge ball is certainly all about having fun. Some of us may remember playing this sport as primary school pupils. Its popularity, however, has led to its being played at other educational levels in many countries. Dodge ball differs greatly from other team sports that use a ball. First of all, there is not just one ball, but several; sometimes as many as ten in play all at once. The balls have to be made of light rubber and filled with air so that they can bounce around the playing areas and not injure other players. Secondly, scoring, if it can be called that, involves hitting another player, resulting in their exit from the round. Be careful, though – if they catch your ball, you're out. The winning team is the one that eliminates all the players from the other team. Generally, the balls cannot be kicked nor can they be thrown at people's heads on purpose. Other rules of the game vary, with some teams making up their own rules.

10 Underline the information in the article which gave you the answers.

Exam focus:
reading for specific information in *First*

1 Look at the exam practice section on pages 12 and 13 and choose the correct answer.

When reading for specific information you should

a scan all the texts to find important pieces of information first.

b read every question, then scan all the texts for all the answers.

c look at one question, then scan for the answer in the texts.

2 Answer each question with the letter of a text, A or B. For some questions, more than one text may be chosen.

Which text includes

1 locations where the sport takes place? ____

2 how many team members participate? ____

3 at least two activities involved in game play? ____

4 players' physical requirements? ____

5 a specific example of teamwork? ____

6 how points are scored? ____

7 a position that players hold? ____

8 how the goal areas are positioned? ____

A Volleyball
Volleyball is a terrific team sport because it's a very active game that is played in a great spot, usually a sandy place on a beach or in a park. The skills required by players involve hitting the ball over the net, either from an up-close position or from a back area. Each player must also know how to be a server and serve the ball to begin a round of game play. In reality, all players must be skilled in each position of the game, as players change positions after each round of play. This gives everyone a chance to participate in the different roles of the sport.

B Basketball
Basketball is a very fast-paced game involving two teams with five players in each team. The players must score points by throwing the ball in one of the two baskets placed at each end of the court. A great deal of teamwork is involved because players must pass the ball to one another frequently throughout the game. The game play goes on continuously, so players use a lot of energy in this sport. It also helps to be tall as the basket is placed three metres high.

3 Underline and write the information in the texts which gave you the answers.

1 _____

2 _____

3 _____

4 _____

5 _____

6 _____

7 _____

8 _____

Skills tip

In *First* Paper 1 Part 7, does scanning for information help us

a determine if a piece of information is NOT in a text? **Yes / No**

b locate information in more than one text? **Yes / No**

Exam practice:
First Paper 1 Part 7

You are going to read an article about four team captains. For questions 1–10, choose from the team captains (A–D). The team captains may be chosen more than once.

Which person

says that encouraging the team is extremely important?	**1** ☐
mentions putting players in positions that they may not like?	**2** ☐
says that he/she will never resort to rudeness?	**3** ☐
has trouble maintaining his/her players' safety?	**4** ☐
makes sure that the game goes according to a pre-arranged plan?	**5** ☐
recognises the players' desire to be well known for what they do?	**6** ☐
reminds players that they are useless if they get hurt?	**7** ☐
is aware that game plans sometimes have to change?	**8** ☐
gives players a few special words prior to a game?	**9** ☐
keeps adequate medical supplies handy?	**10** ☐

Skills tip

When you do *First* Paper 1 Part 7, look at the titles of the separate texts, then look at the first question and make a note of a key word or phrase. Look through the texts for information that's related to that key word or phrase. Each time you find information related to the key word or phrase, read more carefully to find out if it's the correct answer. Continue doing this until you've answered all the questions. Leave enough time at the end to double check that your answers are correct.

TEAM
sports

Four team captains talk about their sport.

A Stephen Hartman – Rugby

Rugby's a pretty tough contact sport, and as such can attract some pretty tough players. In the heat of the game, some of them may want to argue with the referee, but that's no way to play – or win – the match. I'm the only person on my team who can talk to the ref, and I always do that with the utmost politeness and respect, even if I strongly disagree with the call that's been made. I'd say the secret to being a good captain lies in organisational skills. Before the match, I draw up a checklist of the opposing team's strengths and weaknesses, and decide on the main strategy. I need to make sure each player's natural talents will be used to the fullest. During the match, I need to constantly check players are sticking to the strategy we decided on – but without too much micro-management, and being flexible depending on the situation. Ensuring that everyone constantly works as a team is extremely important, because winning's all about group effort.

B Monica Sykes – Basketball

It takes more than just hours of training and practising to defeat your opponents. The main responsibility of a team captain, in my opinion, is to be optimistic that the team can win. So, before every game, I give a little pep talk to the team to motivate them. Players need to hear things like 'This is our game to win,' and 'We can do this'. Of course, it doesn't stop there. Once the whistle blows, I'm out there on the court, doing all the things a leader has to do. I'm there to tell them it's all right when they make a mistake, to give them praise for a job well done, to keep pushing them. That kind of support is essential if you want a chance of winning the league.

C Peter Shawl – Ice Hockey

Ice hockey's a particularly dangerous sport, as anyone who watches it or plays will tell you. Despite all the protective gear we wear – the knee pads, the shin pads, the safety helmets, etc – players can still end up with injuries. With everyone skating at full speed around the rink, it's highly likely that there's going to be some physical contact. And the rules allow us to use our whole body in order to stop an opponent dead in their tracks. One issue I face as team captain is what to do about that. I tell my team to generally play it safe, because what good are they to the rest of the team when they've been carried off on a stretcher? I do my best to make sure their gear's in good shape, that they know what they're doing before they get out on the rink, and that the first-aid kit is well stocked!

D Vera Bedington – Football

Top footballers these days have the money and fame of royalty, and quite a few of the players at my level aspire to be like them. Basically, they all want to be stars! That's great in terms of giving it your all during the game in the quest for personal glory. But one of the things I need to do as a team captain is make sure everyone's playing in the right position. I've got several players who want to be strikers and who want to hold the record for scoring the most goals during the season. They're all terrific players, but I know who the best ones are for each position. A key part of my job is to make tough decisions about their roles when it comes to an important game like a national championship. I have to continually stress to them that it's not just their individual performance but teamwork that wins the game.

Reading for gist

Business travel

Improve your reading skills: reading for gist

What is reading for gist?	*The gist of a text is the general meaning. When you read for gist, you understand the topic of the text and the writer's opinion in general. You don't read to understand the details. Reading for gist is a quick way of reading to find out what a text is about.*

1 When you read for gist, you read

    A slowly to understand each word.

    B quickly to get the general meaning.

Why is reading for gist important?	*It gives us the general meaning of a text quickly. Then, we can decide whether we need to read it in more detail or not. Sometimes, the general meaning is enough but, at other times, we need more information. When you read a review of a film, for example, you might just want to know what kind of film it is and whether it is worth seeing or not. With an article on a website, you might read it for gist first and then go back to read specific parts in detail.*

2 When you read a film review for gist, you find out

    A all the good and bad points about the film.

    B whether the writer recommends the film or not.

How do you read for gist?	*Look at the title of the text and any photos. They often tell you what a text is about. Then, 'skim' the text. This means you read it very quickly, ignoring any words or phrases you don't know. You can usually understand the gist without understanding every single word in a text. Try to focus on 'key words', (words which contain the main meaning) and ignore words which don't particularly add to the main meaning. Also, pay more attention to the first sentence in each paragraph. This is usually the 'topic sentence', which tells you what the paragraph is about.*

3 When you read for gist, what should you do with words you don't understand?

    A Make a note of them for later.

    B Ignore them for now.

How is reading for gist important in *First*?	*Reading for gist is particularly important in* First *Paper 1 Parts 5 and 6 and helps with Part 7. In Part 5, it helps you to understand quickly what the text is about before you look at the questions. It also helps you to answer questions about general meaning and the writer's opinions. In Part 6, reading for gist gives you the overall meaning and logic of the text, which helps you to put the removed sentences in the right places. In Part 7, reading the short texts for gist gives you the general meaning of each one, before reading them in more detail to find specific information.*

4 In *First* Paper 1, reading for gist

    A can help with Parts 5, 6 and 7.

    B is important in Part 7 only.

Get started

Look at the photo and answer the questions.

- Tick the types of business travel that are common in your country.

  travelling abroad on business ☐

  flying to another town/city in the same country on business ☐

  driving long distances to and from work each day ☐

  travelling to and from work by train ☐

  going on long train journeys to business meetings ☐

  driving long distances to business meetings ☐

  other ☐

- Number the following problems business travellers face, ranked in order of how serious you think they are. Put number 1 next to the most serious.

road rage	___	stress	___
delayed or cancelled flights or trains	___	jet lag	___
illness	___	broken routine	___

Develop your vocabulary

1 These words and phrases are all related to travelling.
  Put them in the correct categories. Add two more words or phrases to each category.

  commute ▪ delays ▪ guest house ▪ hotel ▪ jet lag ▪ luggage

Accommodation	Travelling	Problems

2 Circle the word or phrase that does not belong.
  1 to **stay in / go in / travel to / jet off to** a place
  2 to **get to / go on / arrive at / reach** your destination
  3 to **journey / visit London / go away / travel** on business
  4 to be on a **plane / flight / travel / trip**
  5 to **go with the / take the / travel by / use the** train

3 Write a word from the box in each gap.

  exotic ▪ foreign ▪ local ▪ luxurious

Carole says of her time as our senior representative abroad 'I would definitely recommend the travel industry as a career choice. I loved jetting off to (1) _____ locations several times a year. Who wouldn't enjoy staying in (2) _____ five-star hotels where your every need is taken care of? Most of all, I loved finding out more about (3) _____ cultures and getting to meet (4) _____ people. However, it's here at company headquarters in Paris that I feel I really belong.'

Develop your reading skills: reading for gist

1 Read the titles and sub-titles of four newspaper articles. What do you think each article is about?

1

Let the *train* *take the strain*

Jody Sinha looks at the advantages

of leaving your car

at home.

2

Flying **high**

We look at the increase in air travel. The story of how travel really took off in the business world ... and where it might end up.

3

Travelling ## BACK IN TIME

Nearly 200 years ago, Harold Phillipson used to take the train from Radnor to go to work in Philadelphia every day. Amazingly, he wrote it all down in detail. Now, reporter Judith Amundson has been reading the diary of one of the world's first commuters.

4

—KILLER— ## CARS

Driving to work in your car could be killing you – and we're not talking about accidents. The way you sit, the air you breathe and even your car stereo could be harming you! However, it's the way you feel that could be causing you the most damage.

2 Write down any words and phrases you think might appear in the articles in exercise 1.

3 Read the beginnings of two articles about aspects of travel. Match each sentence with an article. Put the sentences in the correct order to complete the paragraphs.

Article 1
When people think of commuting, they usually have a car or train in mind, but few people would think of a bicycle. ...
— — —

Article 2
A new internet service for business travellers promises to take all the stresses and strains out of travelling. ...
— — —

a They also benefit from the savings they make on petrol, car insurance and parking expenses.

b All you have to do is fill in a simple form at troublefreetrips.com and you will receive a package on your computer with vital information on how to get the most out of your trip.

c However, there is a dedicated and growing number of people who sometimes choose to travel long distances to and from work in this way.

d Think of the hours you would spend searching for all that information on different sites.

e This will include travel information, recommended places to stay and visit and even events that are on during your stay.

f They do it because they love the freedom it gives them and also the exercise they get, which helps to compensate for the unhealthy aspects of a desk job.

4 Read only the first sentence in each of the four texts below. What do you think each text will be about?

1

Why spend hours on the road or on the train when you could fly to your meeting in approximately sixty minutes? 'What about the cost?' you say. 'Surely air travel is far too expensive – the accounts department would never agree to it.' Well, we've got good news here, too. We're offering flights from London to Glasgow for just £69 return, if you book in advance. Plus, with our early morning and late evening flights, think of how much you will save in overnight accommodation. Isn't it time to have a word with your accounts department?

2

Just what is it that turns normal people into monsters when they get behind the wheel of a car? We have seen from studies that the people who get stressed and angry while driving do not easily lose their tempers in ordinary everyday situations. Some experts have claimed that people become territorial about the road space their car occupies. If someone invades this, the reaction is an angry one. However, we also have to consider the purpose of the journey. When people are late for an appointment or a meeting, they get annoyed and every little event on the road can cause more anger and stress.

3

Anyone who travels anywhere can become ill, but the frequent business traveller is more at risk than most of us. Stomach problems are the most common, with up to half of all business people reporting at least one such incident in a foreign country. These distressing complaints can sometimes be avoided, if you are careful about what you eat and drink. Experts also advise us to be careful of adding ice in drinks, since the ice may have been made with contaminated water. You should bear this in mind when drinking water, too. Only bottled water will give you a reasonable chance of staying well. There can be few things worse than flying half-way around the world – only to miss an important meeting due to illness.

4

Language is not the only barrier you have to overcome in another country – there are many cultural differences that can stand in the way of doing good business. The business card is a perfect example of this. In the West, we might casually accept someone's card and put it in our pocket. This could cause offence in many parts of Asia, where you are expected to look at it and keep it in sight during your meeting. Also, be careful with your appearance. A smart, clean suit would be the safest look and men should be clean-shaven, too. Remember that in some cultures you are expected to remove your shoes in certain rooms so pay attention to details such as your socks!

5 Read the texts in exercise 4 again and match each text with a heading. There are two extra headings which you do not need to use.

a Respect foreign customs

b *When an accident happens*

c Come fly with us

d Anger on our roads

e Improve your business

f *How to stay well while travelling*

6 Four sentences have been removed from the texts in exercise 4. Put one sentence in the correct place in each text.

a In Asia, these are usually offered and accepted with both hands.
b Doctors recommend avoiding salads, since they may contain the bacteria that cause the problem, or have been washed with water that is not as pure as it should be.
c Think about it – the price of petrol or a return train ticket would cost a great deal more.
d With some drivers it is only a matter of time before these all add up and cause an angry response.

7 Which words and phrases helped you decide?

8 Answer the questions about the texts in exercise 4.
1 What makes some drivers annoyed?
2 Why might ice in drinks be dangerous?
3 Why are socks important to the business traveller?
4 How much does a return flight from London to Glasgow cost?
5 How many business people suffer from stomach problems?
6 What do some people become territorial about?

Exam focus:
reading for gist in *First*

1 Look at the exam practice section on page 20. Read the title and the first sentence of the text and circle the correct answers.

   1 The text is probably mostly about **business people / tourists**.

   2 The writer is likely to focus on **negative aspects only / positive and negative aspects**.

2 Read the text on page 20 for gist and write the numbers of the paragraphs that are *mainly* about these subjects.

   1 Drivers and train passengers ___

   2 Food and exercise ___ ___ ___

   3 Opinions other than the writer's ___ ___ ___

   4 People who fly ___ ___

3 Underline the information in the text which gave you the answers.

4 Look at the numbered gaps in the text below and choose what information (a, b or c) could fit in each gap. Give reasons for your choices.

The hotel is rated five stars and is located just five minutes' walk from the famous Golden Sands Beach. Also within easy walking distance are several excellent cafés and restaurants and we are just a short taxi journey away from the main conference centres and the town centre. **1** ☐	The hotel itself is equipped with all the luxuries the business traveller could wish for, with free wireless broadband access in all rooms and public areas. There is a fully-equipped gym and swimming pool. **2** ☐ We also have a 200-seater restaurant with a range of continental and local dishes on offer daily.

Gap 1

  a a comment about the rooms in the hotel

  b the distances from an airport or train station

  c opening hours of the hotel restaurant

Gap 2

  a something about the history of the hotel

  b something in the town that business travellers would be interested in

  c something else which the hotel offers

5 Write two sentences that could go in the gaps in exercise 4.

   Gap 1 _____

   Gap 2 _____

6 Decide if these statements are true (T) or false (F).

   1 Reading for gist helps you only in Part 6. ___

   2 Reading for gist can help you to quickly understand what the text is about in all parts of Paper 1. ___

   3 Reading for gist can help you to answer general questions about the text in Part 5. ___

   4 Reading for gist can help you to quickly understand the texts in Part 7, before reading them in more detail. ___

> **Skills tip**
>
> In *First* Paper 1 Part 6, does reading for gist help you
>
> **a** identify and locate the different things the writer mentions? **Yes / No**
>
> **b** understand the general theme of the text? **Yes / No**

Exam practice:
First Paper 1 Part 6

You are going to read an article about people who travel for their work. Six sentences have been removed from the article. Choose from the sentences A–G the one which fits each gap (1–6). There is one extra sentence which you do not need to use.

THE BUSINESS
of travelling

Timothy Duke looks at some of the problems business travellers face – and finds some solutions.

To many people, travelling on business sounds glamorous. The idea of jetting off to a foreign country, staying in a luxurious hotel and eating exotic food certainly has an appeal to those who find their working lives routine and boring. The health worries, discomfort and stress tell a different story, however.

We have known for some time that flying through different time zones can cause jet lag. The effects of this vary from simply feeling tired to disorientation or interrupted sleep, sometimes lasting several days. More recent studies have highlighted links between flying and two potentially deadly conditions – increased blood pressure and deep vein thrombosis (DVT), which is thought to be caused by restricted movement, such as that experienced on a long-haul flight. **1**

But frequent flyers are not the only ones who have health concerns. People who take the train or drive long distances to meetings may still suffer from conditions such as DVT. **2** This is your job and you don't want to be late, so any problems such as bad weather or delays are bound to increase your stress levels and we know that that is not healthy.

Another common problem is that, away from home, the business traveller may be forced to rely on less healthy food. While travelling, it's often much easier to buy sweets and snacks than it is to find healthier options such as fruit or a salad. **3**

Fiona Valentine, manager of Valentine Fitness Centre, knows how much business trips can spoil an otherwise healthy lifestyle. Fiona explains, 'Many of our clients lose motivation after a trip. **4** Then, when they return, it's hard for them to get back to a healthy routine.'

But there is a ray of hope for the business traveller. Fiona continues, 'We advise clients on the healthier options on hotel menus. One tactic is to choose the healthiest meal on offer and only eat half a portion. We also suggest buying fruit when you can – or packing some in your luggage. As for exercise, we strongly recommend walking as much as possible. **5** '

And let's not forget that it's nice to travel, even if it is for work. One businessman, Daniel Long, had some good ideas. 'I avoid large hotel chains,' he told me. 'I find them to be pretty much the same everywhere. **6** I would much rather be in a family-run guest house where I can meet local people. Whenever possible, I try to have a free day or two at the beginning or at the end, so I can really get to know the place. Then it's more like a holiday. It takes all the stress out of it.'

A And when they reach their destination, many people also report a temptation to reward themselves with a big meal after their long journey.

B They tell me that they find it impossible to stick to a diet or exercise programme when they're away from home.

C When you think that some business people have to fly many times a year, it is easy to see how the risks could become serious.

D You'd be surprised how many kilometres you can cover inside an airport terminal.

E There are, however, many benefits of foreign travel for business people.

F So I always try to find somewhere to stay which has a bit more character.

G And it is well documented that even a short daily commute to work can raise blood pressure to worrying levels.

Skills tip

When you do *First* Paper 1 Part 6, try to identify what aspect of the topic is being discussed in each section of the text. A new paragraph often (but not always) introduces a slightly different topic. The first sentence of each paragraph usually tells you what the paragraph is about. Sometimes it can indicate a change of topic. The vocabulary in the missing sentence must relate in some way to the topic in that section.

Deducing the meaning of unfamiliar lexical items

Entertainment and media

UNIT AIMS

Skill: deducing the meaning of unfamiliar lexical items

Vocabulary: entertainment topic vocabulary

Exam practice: *First* Paper 1 Part 7

Improve your reading skills: deducing the meaning of unfamiliar lexical items

What is deducing the meaning of unfamiliar lexical items?

Unfamiliar lexical items are words and phrases which you don't know. When you deduce what they mean, you work out what they mean from the context. Sometimes, you can work out exactly what a word or phrase means. More often, however, you can only get a general idea of what a word or phrase means by studying the context.

1 What helps you work out the meaning of words you don't know in a text?
  A the context they appear in
  B a general idea of English words

Why is deducing the meaning of unfamiliar lexical items important?

You can't know every word and phrase in English. Nobody knows every English word! There will always be things you don't understand. It's important to know what to do when that happens. This skill will give you an idea of their meaning and so help you understand the text.

2 Deducing the meaning of unfamiliar lexical items is a skill that
  A native speakers don't need.
  B you will always need.

How do you deduce the meaning of unfamiliar lexical items?

Ignore the words or phrases you don't know and try to understand the gist of the text. Then, work out what part of speech (adjective, noun, etc) the word or phrase is. Read the sentence the word or phrase appears in and consider the general meaning. Is it a positive or negative idea? Does it describe a physical action or a mental action? Can you think of other words and phrases that seem to fit there? Try to get as close to the meaning as you can.

3 If you can only get a general idea of the meaning of a word or phrase,
  A you won't be able to understand the text.
  B it can still be very useful.

How is deducing the meaning of unfamiliar lexical items important in *First*?

Deducing the meaning of unfamiliar lexical items is important in First *Paper 1 Parts 5, 6 and 7. In all these parts of the exam, trying to understand words and phrases you don't know will help you do the tasks. In Part 5, it helps you to select the correct answers to the multiple choice questions. In Part 6, it helps you to understand connections between the text and the removed sentences. And in Part 7, deducing unfamiliar lexical items will help you understand specific information, so you can do the matching task.*

4 In *First* Paper 1 Part 6, deducing the meaning of unfamiliar lexical items
  A helps you see links between the text and the removed sentences.
  B helps you see why each sentence has been removed.

Get started

Look at the photo and answer the questions.

- How do you listen to music and watch television or films?
- What is your favourite type of entertainment and why?

Develop your vocabulary

1 Write a word from the box in each gap to complete the sentences.

> fan ■ industry ■ judging ■ media ■ networking ■ red-carpet

1 I'd love to work in the entertainment _____ after university – my ambition is to become a television executive.

2 The actress attracted unwanted _____ attention after she was involved in a political scandal.

3 The band has a huge _____ base, who follow all their activities on Twitter.

4 She caused a media sensation when she appeared at the _____ event in a gold designer dress.

5 I love using social _____ sites – I have accounts on Twitter, Facebook and Flickr.

6 The show's _____ panel is made up of one music producer, two pop singers and a celebrity TV presenter.

2 Read the paragraph and circle the correct words.

> Not every actor will end up being a (**1**) **celebrity / famous**, constantly in the public (**2**) **sight / eye**. Most begin their careers working in the theatre, where they learn their craft. It's important to develop the ability to give a good (**3**) **act / performance** night after night, even if you are wearing a heavy stage (**4**) **suit / costume** that's difficult to move in. But these are problems that all (**5**) **talented / suitable** performers learn to overcome. And though world-wide fame may be hard to achieve, theatre (**6**) **spectators / audiences** always appreciate good acting.

3 Match the words in bold with their synonyms.

1 What time do they **broadcast** the news on the BBC in the evening? ___

2 Angry **viewers** voted her off the reality TV show. ___

3 The show's **ratings** have improved since Andy Crouch took on the lead role – seven million viewers now tune in to watch each episode. ___

4 Kate got a job as a **TV producer** on a new celebrity cooking programme. ___

5 She's so famous that the **paparazzi** follow her everywhere. ___

a viewing figures, number of people who watch a show
b person who makes a TV show
c transmit, show on TV
d people who watch TV
e photographers who follow celebrities and take their photos

Develop your reading skills:
deducing the meaning of unfamiliar lexical items

1 Match the words in bold with the correct parts of speech.

  1 The applause was **deafening** as the curtain came down.
The audience loved the play.   ——

  2 I'm not having much luck **booking** a seat for the ballet.
The tickets are sold out.   ——

  3 *Homeland* is a series with very high viewer **ratings** in the
UK – the final episode was watched by 2.8 million people. ——

  4 She managed to perform in the concert **despite** feeling
very unwell. After the show she went back to bed.   ——

  5 She was **tremendously** pleased with the positive
reviews of her novel.   ——

  a noun
  b adjective
  c verb
  d adverb
  e conjunction

2 Can you deduce the meaning of the words in bold in exercise 1?
Circle the most suitable answer.

  1 *deafening* means **very loud / very quiet**
  2 *booking* a seat means **reserving a ticket / finding somewhere to sit**
  3 *ratings* means **interactive participation / how many people watch a show**
  4 *despite* means **because / although**
  5 *tremendously* means **not very / very**

3 Read the paragraph and answer the questions.

> The theatre group Moving On was **set up** in 2012 to work with young unemployed people in the community. The idea was to put on performances relating to **issues** that young people face in their everyday lives. Playwright Danielle Abela is closely involved with the project. 'I had 13 weeks to write and **stage** a play with a group of enthusiastic but inexperienced teenagers. We wanted to **tackle** the negative image that so many adults have of teenagers today. Our project gives young people the chance to prove that they have **an awful lot** to offer their local community. The great thing was that the whole team, the kids and everyone else involved, just **threw themselves into it**.'

1 When did the theatre group begin?
2 What is the subject of the group's shows?
3 Does Danielle's involvement include writing only, or writing and directing?
4 What does Danielle say about adults' view of young people?
5 According to Danielle, do young people offer something negative or positive to their community?
6 What does Danielle say about the team's work?

4 Write the words and phrases in bold from exercise 3 next to their definitions.
Use your answers from exercise 3 to help you deduce the meaning of the words.

1 deal with something difficult   _____

2 problems   _____

3 a large amount   _____

4 put on, direct   _____

5 used a lot of energy   _____

6 start, establish   _____

5 Decide if the words and phrases in bold
have a positive (P) or a negative (N) meaning.

1 John **made a** complete **fool of himself**
at the party – it was so embarrassing!

___

2 Her performance was a **show-stopper**
and got fantastic reviews in the press.

___

3 The play was a box-office **flop** and
closed after just four weeks.

___

4 The plot is **intriguing** and will
keep you on the edge of your seat.

___

5 With such a **star-studded** cast,
audiences are sure to flock to the film.

___

6 What do the phrases in bold mean?
Choose the best answer.

1 She loves **being in the limelight**,
posing for pictures and giving interviews.
  a leading a quiet life
  b being the centre of media attention
  c organising other people

2 The lead actor is ill and many of the
costumes don't fit but **the show must go on**.
  a we can never give up
  b the situation is hopeless
  c we need to find more costumes

3 He **stole the show** with his astonishing
dance skills.
  a he ruined the whole performance
  b he was the best performer
  c he upset the other performers

4 I'm **running the show** here, so
stop interfering and do as you're told!
  a I insist people work together
  b I don't have much time
  c I'm the person in charge

5 It was a magnificent performance and
the final scene **brought the house down**.
  a made the audience very angry
  b received wild applause
  c caused the stage to collapse

Exam focus:
deducing the meaning of unfamiliar lexical items

1 Look at the exam practice section on pages 28 and 29 and tick the statements that are true.
Being able to deduce the meaning of unfamiliar lexical items …

1 is a skill which only the best students can develop. ____

2 requires you to completely understand all the words in a text. ____

3 will help you to understand the texts better as a whole. ____

4 can help you to identify synonyms in a text. ____

5 takes up too much valuable time for little or no result. ____

6 is one of the ways that will help you to identify which text a question refers to. ____

2 Read the paragraph and match the words and phrases in bold with
their synonyms. Do NOT use a dictionary to help you.

> In comparison with only a few years ago, the price of tablet PCs has **plunged**. With the latest models on offer at such low prices, many people have decided to **invest in** one. They don't think it's such a major **extravagance** either. In fact, they view it as a necessity. You can download books, films and music onto it and it performs many other useful **functions** as well. Once you have one, you'll find it hard to imagine how you ever managed without it – it will quickly become an **essential** part of your life.

1	**plunged**	**a**	tasks	____
2	**invest in**	**b**	fallen dramatically	____
3	**extravagance**	**c**	very important	____
4	**functions**	**d**	buy	____
5	**essential**	**e**	waste of money	____

Skills tip

In *First* Paper 1 Part 7, should you try to deduce the meaning of unfamiliar lexical items

a by looking only at the sentence in which the item occurs? **Yes / No**

b by looking at the context of both the sentence and the rest of the paragraph?

Yes / No

3 Look at exercise 2 again. Which of these strategies helped
you to guess the meaning of the unknown words and phrases?

1 trying to guess from context what the synonym could be ____

2 replacing the unknown words with a synonym (from
the list a–e) to see if the sentence still made sense ____

3 looking for a word or phrase with a related meaning
shortly before or after the unknown word ____

4 Which statement best describes the ability to deduce the meaning of unfamiliar lexical items?

a It's a skill that can help you in many parts of *First* Paper 1.

b It's a skill with little benefit in an exam setting.

c It can only help you in one part of *First* Paper 1.

Exam practice:
First **Paper 1** Part 7

You are going to read an article about attitudes to the world of entertainment.
For questions 1–10, choose from the people (A–D). The people may be chosen more than once.

Which person

plans with others how to get the results they want?	**1** ☐
mentions setbacks that have affected part of the entertainment industry?	**2** ☐
feels an industry took the wrong approach to modern developments at first?	**3** ☐
says that in his/her industry consumers used to accept whatever was offered to them?	**4** ☐
comments on the presentation of entertainment acts?	**5** ☐
finds it difficult to separate their home life from their work?	**6** ☐
emphasises what they have to do to maintain their position in the industry?	**7** ☐
says technological advances have changed how people consume entertainment?	**8** ☐
emphasises the need for fresh ideas to keep people interested?	**9** ☐
tries to involve their followers in what they do as much as possible?	**10** ☐

Skills tip

In *First* Paper 1 Part 7, it's a good idea to read through the questions before you read the texts to help you think about the kind of information you need to identify. You can underline key words and phrases in the questions to help you look out for synonyms in the text. When reading through the texts, underline the words, phrases and ideas you think relate to the questions and compare them with the key words you have identified in the questions. Remember that you don't have to understand every single word in the texts in order to be able to complete this task successfully.

BREAKING NEW GROUND
in entertainment

A The television executive

Like myself, most television executives look back fondly to a golden age when viewers were happy to schedule their leisure hours around the broadcast times of their favourite TV series. But those days are gone; audiences today are far more sophisticated and no longer accept the idea of being spoon-fed their entertainment. The television industry has had to adapt to this new climate of viewer-led broadcasting. Although costume dramas and crime series still achieve good ratings, in order to stay ahead of the game, television producers have to constantly find new shows to attract advertisers. Audiences become bored with the same game shows, talent shows and reality TV shows after a while, so you have to come up with exciting new formats to keep the viewers tuned in.

B The actress

Finding work as an actress is about keeping yourself in the public eye. It's no longer simply a case of being well-trained in the dramatic arts; the job also involves a great deal of self-promotion. For example, if I'm lucky enough to be invited to a red-carpet event, I have to put on a good show for the paparazzi to make sure I get plenty of media attention. Social networking sites such as Twitter can be useful in that respect, too – I use Twitter to publicise my work and to keep my fan base up to date with all my activities. You have to interact with your fans and let them feel that they're a part of the entertainment world, too. It does mean, though, that I have to be very careful about striking a balance between being a celebrity and a private person, which can be very challenging sometimes!

C The viewer

I'm a big fan of talent shows. They're great fun to watch and I love being involved in the whole judging process. Just before the show is broadcast, I log on to a live blog for the show and while the performers are on stage, I blog about whether the performance is any good, what the costumes are like and if they're talented or not. I feel very involved and it's tremendous fun. I like the fact that television is much more interactive these days – as a viewer you can really feel a part of the whole process. The shows aren't just in the hands of the TV judging panel – the audience has power as well. That's what makes it such fun. I enjoy voting off the judges' favourites. I discuss tactical voting strategies with other bloggers and we do our best to help our favourites win!

D The record producer

The music industry had no sooner recovered from the effects of technological developments such as CDs and DVDs, than another hi-tech leap forward knocked it off its feet again. The latest threat is the unstoppable rise of new social networking sites as well as devices such as smartphones and tablet PCs, which give people easy access to those sites. Instead of going out to buy music from a shop, people are simply downloading MP3 files straight from the net onto their devices. In the industry we were very slow to adapt to the new ways in which people use technology to access entertainment. It's easy to understand why. For years, music moguls had total control over the products they sold until, almost overnight, that all ended. We tried to stamp out activities such as downloading music or uploading videos onto YouTube. Then it dawned on us that music videos are a good promotional strategy for bands. There's an old saying: 'If you can't beat them, join them' and this is what we in the music industry have started to do. Today, a future that had seemed in doubt is much more secure.

4

Distinguishing main ideas from supporting details

Applying for a job

Improve your reading skills: distinguishing main ideas from supporting details

What is distinguishing main ideas from supporting details?

A text usually contains a small number of main ideas. Each main idea may be supported by examples, reasons, further information and other supporting details. To fully understand a text, you need to be able to see what a main idea is and what a supporting detail is. It is an important part of understanding the structure of a text.

1 Which of the following is not a supporting detail?

   A a summary of the whole text

   B an explanation of the reasons why something is true

Why is distinguishing main ideas from supporting details important?

When you read, it's important to understand the structure of the text. It helps you to pay attention to the most important things. Part of that is distinguishing main ideas from supporting details. The main ideas show you the key points in the text. The supporting details show you why the writer believes the main ideas. Understanding both of these things is an important part of understanding the text as a whole.

2 Supporting details help you to understand

   A why you are reading a text.

   B the reasons for the writer's opinions.

How do you distinguish main ideas from supporting details?

You need to understand what kind of information (examples, reasons, etc) is usually presented as supporting details. Look out for this kind of information and see what it refers to. Pay particular attention to the first sentence of each paragraph, which is often the 'topic sentence' (although sometimes the topic sentence may appear later in the paragraph). This usually makes a main point, which the rest of the paragraph then supports. Make a note of all the main points, together with any supporting details provided. Compare this to the structure of the text as a whole.

3 It helps if you know that examples and reasons are usually

   A main points.

   B supporting details.

How is distinguishing main ideas from supporting details important in *First*?

Distinguishing main ideas from supporting details is particularly important in First *Paper 1 Parts 5 and 6 and helps with Part 7. In Part 5, it helps you to answer questions on the way the text is organised and other features of the text, such as examples. In Part 6, it helps you understand the structure of the text. Then, you can see how each removed sentence fits into the text structure. In Part 7, you may need to understand supporting details in order to do the matching task.*

4 How does distinguishing main ideas from supporting details help in Part 6?

   A You can see how each removed sentence relates to the whole text.

   B You can see examples of sentences that have been removed.

Get started

Look at the photo and answer the questions.

- What might the woman on the right have done to reach this interview?
- Which of these emotions might the woman be feeling? Why?

> angry ▪ bored ▪ excited ▪ nervous ▪ pleased

- What do you think might happen next?

Develop your vocabulary

1 Match to make phrases.

1	job	___	**a**	form
2	learning	___	**b**	market
3	careers	___	**c**	counsellor
4	application	___	**d**	packet
5	pay	___	**e**	curve

2 Write a word from the box in each gap to complete the sentences.

> apply ▪ attend ▪ gain ▪ land ▪ offers ▪ send

1 You can _____ valuable experience taking a summer job in an office.

2 If you _____ for a job, make sure you research the company carefully.

3 After months of trying, Tony finally managed to _____ a job.

4 Jean was ill, so she couldn't _____ the interview she'd been preparing for.

5 My advice is to _____ out as many applications as you can.

6 You will probably have to fill in dozens of application forms before a company _____ you a job.

3 Read the paragraph and circle the correct words.

> ■ ☒
>
> Dear Alan,
>
> A new job **(1) chance / opportunity** has just come up that we feel is ideal for you. The **(2) employee / employer** is opening new offices in the north-east, which could mean fast growth and rapid **(3) promotion / qualification** for someone willing to work hard. Please note, however, that this is an entry-level **(4) position / location** and as such you should not expect to be offered a very high **(5) post / salary**. Have a closer look at the advertisement online at www.starrecruitment.co.uk and, if you are interested, send me an up-to-date **(6) CV / PS** and a covering letter explaining why you are suitable for the job.
>
> With best wishes,
> Deborah Willis
> Star Recruitment

Develop your reading skills:
distinguishing main ideas from supporting details

1 Read the text and label the underlined sentences. You will use one of the letters twice.

   a supporting reason
   b example
   c topic sentence

1 ___

2 ___

3 ___

4 ___

That's not the only point. Managers will often put a CV on the rejection pile for any number of reasons. This is not something one should take personally. It happens because they will receive hundreds of applications for a job and need a way to cut that number down quickly to the twenty or so they intend to interview. The list is obviously endless, but includes major gaps, such as lack of qualifications, and minor oversights, such as spelling errors.

2 Match each topic sentence with a supporting detail.

   1 Very few people in a new job could carry out their duties perfectly from the start. ___

   2 It is worth doing a course, if that skill is in great demand at present. ___

   3 Latest figures show record unemployment for 16-year-old school leavers. ___

   4 This particular recruitment agency has a remarkable record of filling job vacancies. ___

   5 There are lists of standard interview questions on the internet. ___

   a This has been put down to the current economic climate, which shows no sign of improving.
   b The main reason for this is that they make sure their recommended candidates are suitable.
   c Employers understand that there is a learning curve in every position.
   d An obvious example is computer literacy, which is a must in every office nowadays.
   e These include classics like 'What's your greatest weakness?' and candidates should have an answer prepared.

3 Match the paragraphs with the topic sentences.
There is one extra sentence which you do not need to use.

   1 ___ No-one is expecting an interviewee to grin manically throughout the interview, but there's nothing worse than a blank or worried expression. Here's an old trick: looking up at the ceiling and raising your eyebrows just before entering the interview room will relax your face.

   2 ___ Interviewers spend all day listening to answers to the same set of questions, and so they would appreciate someone who is concise. Also, digressing into an anecdote about your Aunt Sandy doesn't say much for your ability to focus on one task. If you have a relevant story to tell, practise it until you can deliver it in as few words as possible.

   3 ___ Scratching the nose or breaking eye contact, for example, are both sure signs that the interviewee is not being entirely honest. Someone who does not sit straight might be lazy, while someone who sits too straight is probably not creative. These are subjective and perhaps hasty judgements, but interviewers are human, like everyone else.

   a Your face should be open and friendly, inviting conversation from the interviewer.
   b Small details, such as posture, or the way you hold your head, have a greater impact than you can imagine.
   c One interviewer we surveyed said she pays a lot of attention to a candidate's body language.
   d Candidates should keep their answers to the point, without being monosyllabic.

4 Write a word or phrase from the article in each gap to complete the sentences.

Modern failures?

UK companies are complaining that more and more school leavers that apply to them for jobs lack the basics in education. 'I need security guards who can write short reports,' said Tina Hutton, personnel manager at Failsafe Security. 'When some of them try to spell, they come up with words that not even a computer spellchecker would recognise!' Young people today rely on word processor programs that autocorrect and cannot even do simple arithmetic without a calculator to help them. Many teachers blame this dependency on modern technology for falling standards among school leavers. As a result, many firms are putting potential interviewees through a series of tests before they even talk to them.

1 The article is about young people who apply for jobs without having a basic _____ .

2 Many of them can't _____ or do _____ .

3 The reason given is that they depend too much on _____ .

4 Because of this, companies sometimes only interview candidates after they have sat some _____ .

5 Write 'MI' for main idea or 'SD' for supporting detail.

1 If you don't produce a good covering letter, that might be as far as the application process goes.   ___

The covering letter is the first thing that an employer will read.   ___

2 Getting their first job is one of those moments everyone remembers.   ___

It's likely to be something like a papergirl or a waiter, but you still feel a real thrill.   ___

3 It's partly because he's lazy, but he has also had some extremely bad luck.   ___

My brother hasn't had a steady job for over three years and no job at all for the past twelve months.   ___

4 Benefits of the position include one free meal every shift and tips.   ___

We have an opening for a waiter to cover evening shifts at our busy seaside hotel.   ___

6 Each of these paragraphs includes supporting details.
Match each paragraph with a statement showing the role of the supporting detail.

1 I always made sure I kept all my applications carefully and systematically filed away. That way, I never got confused even if I was dealing with twenty of them simultaneously, all at different stages. ___

2 Job satisfaction should be uppermost in a graduate's mind when considering what jobs to apply for. Big pay packets might be tempting, but in the end nothing can compare to a contented working life. ___

3 Many of today's school leavers are finding themselves jobless within twelve months of leaving school. They include Leo Mann, who left at sixteen, expecting to find work on a building site, but is now considering returning to college. ___

4 Laura's father owns a large shipping company and she had a position waiting for her. That's why she could swan off on a round-the-world trip after the exams, while we applied for job after job. ___

a giving an example of the main idea
b expanding on the main idea
c giving a reason for the main idea
d giving a consequence of the main idea

7 Read the article and answer the questions.

Graduating to robbery?

Tom McGregor, 23, walked into the Leith Street branch of the National Bank at 11am on Friday and demanded money at gunpoint. After emptying the cashiers' tills of £15,000, he left and attempted to make his getaway on foot. Unfortunately for him, he ran straight into two police officers, who arrested him. McGregor explained that he had been unable to find a job since graduating from university and poverty had forced him into this desperate act. The gun turned out to be a replica.

1 Who robbed the bank?
2 When did he rob it?
3 How much did he steal?
4 What happened to him after he left the bank?
5 What makes McGregor an unusual bank robber?
6 Why did he rob the bank?

8 Write a topic sentence to complete the gap in the article in exercise 7.

Exam focus:
distinguishing main ideas from supporting details in *First*

1 Look at the exam practice section on pages 36 and 37 and circle the correct word or phrase in each sentence.

1 You will find the main idea of each paragraph near the ***beginning / end***.

2 A supporting idea comes ***before / after*** the main idea.

3 ***Examples / Reasons*** might follow these words and phrases: *like, such as, including*.

4 ***Examples / Reasons*** might follow these words and phrases: *because, since, in order to*.

5 Knowing the main point of a paragraph would definitely help answer questions about ***why the writer said something / the point the writer is trying to make***.

Skills tip

In *First* Paper 1 Part 5, should you underline the topic sentences in the passage

a while you are reading through it for the first time?   **Yes / No**

b after you have read it and the questions once?   **Yes / No**

---

2 Read the text and underline the topic sentence.

Being the best candidate for the job is one thing. That alone is not of much help, however, if you cannot persuade your potential employer that no-one else can do the job better than you. This applies to the entire process, from sending your CV to attending the interview. You must shine at all stages, because your qualifications might impress them enough to get your foot in the door, but that could be as far as you will go. If you show a lack of vital personal qualities, such as a smart appearance and good communication skills, the interviewer will conclude that you are unlikely to be able to fit well into the company structure.

3 Read the text in exercise 2 again and choose the correct answer.

The point the writer is trying to emphasise is that

a it is important to create an impressive CV.

b your performance in the interview makes a strong impression.

c you know that no other candidate is equal to you.

d you must use every opportunity to prove your suitability.

4 Complete these sentences with the answers you did NOT use in exercise 3.

1 You will not be offered a job just because ____

2 In order to make it to the interview stage, ____

3 The way you look and speak is important because ____

5 Complete each statement with *Part 6* or *Part 7*.

In *First* Paper 1, distinguishing main ideas from supporting details

1 will help you to find what kind of sentence is missing in _____ .

2 will give you a way to break down short texts quickly in _____ .

3 will help you find the right answer when the gap is a topic sentence in _____ .

Exam practice:
First Paper 1 Part 5

You are going to read an article about a graduate looking for her first job. For questions 1–6, choose the answer (A, B, C or D) which you think best fits according to the text.

OUT INTO THE
big wide world

Today's graduates are entering one of the toughest job markets in decades. Sylvia Morgan writes about how she finally landed that crucial first post.

I was by no means typical among my peers, but I feel I was well organised in my approach to job hunting. Even before graduation, when many of my friends were enjoying what they termed their 'final year of freedom', I was attending career fairs and getting an idea of which companies were hiring in my chosen field – publishing. I had some sit-down meetings with representatives at the fairs and distributed my CV, but even then there was a feeling of 'let's wait and see'. Nobody wanted to commit and none of the companies seemed sure they would even have jobs to offer in the summer, assuming I graduated with the degree my lecturers expected from me.

I did, but found myself back home in July feeling I was starting again from square one. Although I had taken a short holiday straight after leaving university, I had spent it looking through newspaper job advertisements and online job sites. There had been very little movement in the publishing field and when I got home and found that none of the companies I had contacted before graduating were prepared to make a job offer, I made the pragmatic decision to widen my focus considerably.

I approached job hunting, as much as possible, as a job in itself. Monday to Friday, I put in nine-to-five days (with a break for lunch) filling out online application forms, sending out CVs and following leads. If something looked promising, I was prepared to work overtime in order to exploit the opportunity fully. When I got an interview, I did my homework as a sales representative on a business trip would: researching the company, plotting a sales strategy and trying to put myself in the potential employer's shoes by asking myself questions such as 'What are *they* looking for?'

So the interviews did start coming. There would have been many more, however, if I hadn't had a strict rule; I refused any that even hinted at working as an unpaid intern. These positions are becoming more and more common in the UK, which I think is an extremely damaging trend. Not only do young people nowadays get into debt to obtain a degree, but they also have to be prepared to work for six months or a year without remittance, in the hope of a position with a salary at the end of it. Certainly, you gain experience in the good positions of this kind, but in many you may end up as a glorified coffee maker.

Rejection is something you have to prepare yourself for mentally. First of all, because you will, in all likelihood, receive many of those dreaded emails (or letters, occasionally) before you get the break you are looking for. Secondly, because no matter how strong your self-confidence is, those brief polite sentences will eventually dent it. I strongly advise you not to walk that path alone. Compare notes with university friends and you will find many are going through the same thing. Without my friends, I would have felt like a failure and then I'd never have got a job.

Because I did, eventually, find someone who was prepared to overlook my lack of experience and appreciate my qualifications, I was offered a job and I accepted it. It was after 139 applications – I kept careful count. The starting salary isn't wonderful, but it's a young, fast-moving company with good opportunities for promotion. Three months on, I could look back at my six months of unemployment as a waste of time, but I prefer to see it as a learning curve and a growth experience. This is the real world and the more leisurely life of academic development, careers counselling and self-discovery at university is over.

1 From the first paragraph, we understand that
   A Sylvia feels like she missed out on a lot of opportunities at university.
   B many of Sylvia's fellow students didn't focus on job-hunting before graduation.
   C the job fairs Sylvia attended led to some promising possibilities.
   D Sylvia wishes she had done more to obtain a job pre-graduation.

2 After returning home from her holiday, Sylvia
   A decided to start applying to publishing companies from the beginning.
   B realised that she had been applying for jobs that she wasn't qualified for.
   C immediately began searching newspapers and websites for jobs.
   D switched to a more realistic approach to job-hunting.

3 What point is Sylvia making in the third paragraph?
   A Sales jobs are very often the hardest ones to get.
   B Your approach to finding a job must be professional.
   C You should be prepared to do overtime even when unpaid.
   D How you find a job shows how well you will do in it.

4 What does the word 'remittance' mean in the fourth paragraph?
   A qualifications
   B experience
   C pay
   D duties

5 When a job application ends in rejection, Sylvia believes you should
   A share the experience with people who can empathise.
   B not allow it to do the slightest damage to your self-image.
   C treat it as a valuable lesson in self-reliance.
   D be prepared to examine your preconceptions about yourself.

6 How does Sylvia feel about the time she spent looking for work?
   A nostalgic about her university days
   B determined never to let it happen again
   C disappointed it didn't lead to a better job
   D positive that it taught her a valuable lesson

Skills tip

Beware of the wrong options – they are not called 'distractors' for nothing. They are trying to trick you into choosing them, so they will often correspond to something in the text. They might say the exact opposite, only be half-right or not say quite the same thing. They may even be all right and simply not answer the question that is being asked. Once you have identified the main idea of a paragraph, you can often rule out one or more of these options. Use this as a method of focusing on the answer to the more difficult questions.

5

Understanding
purpose and function

Vegetarianism

UNIT AIMS

Skill: understanding purpose and function

Vocabulary: food and drink topic vocabulary

Exam practice: *First* Paper 1 Part 5

Improve your reading skills: understanding purpose and function

What is understanding purpose and function?	*A writer writes a text for a reason. It might be to entertain, inform or persuade their readers. It might be because they want to make arrangements or offer advice. The reason for writing is the purpose. A piece of writing also has a function, similar to the writer's purpose. The function might be to entertain people, to give people information, etc.*

1 Which of these statements is true?

  A A piece of writing has a function.

  B All pieces of writing try to entertain.

Why is understanding purpose and function important?	*To fully understand a text, you need to know why it was written and what it is trying to say. Understanding the purpose and function helps you to know what to expect when reading. Also, when you understand a writer's purpose and a text's function, you can judge how successful it is. If the purpose is to persuade, do you find it persuasive? If the purpose and function is to entertain, is it entertaining?*

2 Understanding the purpose and function of a text helps you to

  A read about what you know.

  B judge how good the text is.

How do you understand purpose and function?	*Make sure you are familiar with the usual purposes and functions associated with different kinds of texts. For example, the purpose and function of a story may be to entertain or to amuse. It probably isn't to recommend or to inform. Then, ask yourself questions as you read. Why did the writer write this? Who is it aimed at? What was the purpose?*

3 The example of a story is used to show that

  A very few writers know how to write stories well.

  B some text types and some purposes and functions often go together.

How is understanding purpose and function important in *First*?	*Understanding purpose and function is most useful in Paper 1 Part 5. In this part, you may be asked questions about the writer's purpose or the function of the text. You may also be asked questions about who the target reader is, which is closely related to the purpose and function of a text. Some parts of the matching task in Paper 1 Part 7 may also rely on an understanding of the purpose and function of the texts.*

4 What is connected to the purpose and function of a text?

  A the target reader

  B asking questions about a text

Get started

Read the statements and write 'A' if you agree or 'D' if you disagree.

- Vegetarian food is boring and not very appealing.   ___

- All vegetarian food is completely healthy.   ___

- It's relatively easy to follow a vegetarian diet.   ___

- Vegetarians lead a much healthier lifestyle.   ___

Develop your vocabulary

1 Each of the words in bold is in the wrong sentence. Write a word in bold from another sentence to replace the incorrect one.

1 An excellent way to cook vegetables is to **boil** them in a shallow pan with a little olive oil.   _____

2 After placing the potatoes in the baking tray, put them in the oven and **steam** them for one hour.   _____

3 When you **roast** vegetables, you get dark, evenly spaced lines across the surface.   _____

4 The healthiest way to cook food is to **sauté** it over a pan of water.   _____

5 People who **grill** a lot of fatty foods often have weight problems.   _____

6 The recipe says to **consume** the pasta for ten minutes.   _____

2 Write a word from the box in each gap to complete the text.

> dietary ■ dressing ■ greasy ■ savoury ■ spicy ■ sprinkle ■ tasteless ■ tinned ■ vegan

Many people have successfully made the change to vegetarianism. It's certainly harder for some than others. If you're used to having a steaming hot meat stew or a juicy steak for dinner then this change in your (**1**) _____ habits may be difficult. However, it *is* possible to maintain a vegetarian diet and there is a wide variety of recipes available for both sweet and (**2**) _____ dishes. Vegetables can be delicious, if you learn how to cook them properly. It's important to use fresh olive oil and to (**3**) _____ the food with herbs and spices, such as basil, oregano or black pepper. Salads do not have to be boring and (**4**) _____, as long as you add the right kind of (**5**) _____ and the right amount of it. If you like a bit of heat in your food, try adding (**6**) _____ tomato sauce, which is a terrific vegetarian addition to many meals. Of course, even a vegetarian meal can be unhealthy. Frying vegetables in oil makes them quite (**7**) _____ and this is not to everyone's taste. Go easy on the creamy sauces as well, since they're usually full of butter, cream and cheese, unless of course you're (**8**) _____ and don't eat any dairy products either. It's also best to stick with fresh fruit and vegetables, so avoid the supermarket aisle with the (**9**) _____ food and spend more time in the fresh produce section.

Develop your reading skills: understanding purpose and function

1 Match each type of text with a purpose.

1 email	___	**a** to educate people about a subject
2 news article	___	**b** to inform the public about something that recently happened
3 personal blog	___	**c** to persuade someone to do or buy something
4 novel	___	**d** to communicate with another person
5 report	___	**e** to express feelings about a subject
6 advert	___	**f** to publish the findings of a study
7 encyclopaedia	___	**g** to share personal information with many people
8 opinion article	___	**h** to entertain a reader

2 Write a text type from exercise 1 after these introductory sentences.

1 I find it disgusting to see a steak on a plate – what about the poor animal? _____

2 Having fresh vegetables delivered to your home has never been easier with our new online delivery service, Garden at Home. _____

3 I'm writing to tell you about this terrific organic food fair I attended last weekend. _____

4 The soybean is a species of plant that is native to parts of eastern Asia and is grown for its many different uses. _____

5 Research shows that a vegetarian diet can provide just as much protein as a traditional diet, but comes with a much lower fat and cholesterol content. _____

6 Margaret Pace, a born and bred city dweller, grew tired of the hustle and bustle of Johannesburg and opted for a quiet life managing a citrus farm in the countryside. _____

3 Decide if the sentences about the short paragraphs are true (T) or false (F).

1 This was written for a large audience. ___

> I think it's great that you want to start following a vegetarian diet and I can help you to get started, if you like. Do you want to meet sometime and talk more about it?

2 The person wrote this sentence for an encyclopaedia article. ___

> There are many reasons why a person may choose to follow a vegetarian diet and those reasons include ethical and moral beliefs, dietary concerns and religion.

3 The writer wrote this sentence for personal reasons. ___

> Sorry it's been so long since my last communication, but I've been on an exciting month-long volunteering adventure at an organic farm in the countryside.

4 This could be found in a magazine or an advert or heard on a television programme. ___

> Tired of feeling exhausted all the time? Have you put on a few extra pounds that seem impossible to lose? Are you sick of eating tinned food all the time? Perhaps it's time you gave the Raw Foods Challenge a try and put an end to those worries.

5 This person is expressing an opinion. ___

> It's high time that we got our produce out of the hands of scientists, out of laboratories, in which a hundred different tomatoes are grown to look exactly alike.

6 This sentence could be found in a research report. ___

> In a letter to the country's agriculture minister, environmentalists expressed outrage over the ministry's decision to allow factories to open in the farming heartland.

4 Read the articles and label them *story, news article, opinion article* or *persuasive article*.

a

I've never been keen on eating meat. First of all, I'm not fond of the taste, the look or the smell of it. It might have something to do with the way I was brought up. My parents were vegetarians, so there was never any meat in the house. However, I also feel that eating meat is a form of violence against animals. I think that animals are kind, innocent creatures that deserve our respect. In fact, I think killing them should be a crime.

_____

c

A recent report highlights the environmental impact that meat-based diets have on farmland. It has been determined that a plot of land can produce many more times the amount of food in grains, fruit and vegetables than if the same plot of land was supporting farm animals. Additionally, the amount of water used to grow plants is far less than the amount needed to maintain a population of cattle, sheep or even chickens.

_____

b

We really need to do more to rethink our eating habits and there's evidence to show that this need is now urgent. We all know by now that meat products use far more resources than non-meat products. Pretty soon we won't have enough resources for the production of meat and that should be enough to change anybody's mind. Wouldn't it be better if we switched to vegetarianism now, rather than wait until we have no choice?

_____

d

It was Jill's second week of staying on a meat-free diet and she thought that she wouldn't be able to stand it for a minute longer. She never used to crave things such as hamburgers and hot dogs that much before, but now that she had decided not to eat them anymore, she couldn't seem to think of anything else. She also used to love all kinds of vegetables and vegetable dishes. But she was beginning to feel that if she never saw another vegetable in her life that would be just fine by her.

_____

5 Who might be the target reader for the texts in exercise 4?
Write the correct letter. More than one answer may be possible.

1 an environmentalist   _____

2 someone who thinks more people should be vegetarians   _____

3 people who consume too much meat   _____

4 a person reading for entertainment   _____

5 a scientist   _____

6 people finding it difficult to become vegetarians   _____

6 Match the articles from exercise 4 with the purposes below.
More than one answer may be possible. Not all the purposes match an article.

1 to inform   _____   6 to persuade   _____

2 to educate   _____   7 to describe   _____

3 to entertain   _____   8 to advertise   _____

4 to express feelings _____   9 to advise   _____

5 to argue an issue   _____   10 to warn   _____

7 Read the sentences and choose the function of the second sentence.

1 Many people think strict vegetarian diets are unhealthy. The truth is that they can provide the same essential nutrients as a traditional diet, but often with less fat and fewer calories.

   a to clarify a fact
   b to give an opinion

2 Aubergines are a delicious vegetable but many people don't like their bitter taste. To get rid of this taste, it's necessary to soak them in salty water for thirty minutes before cooking.

   a to warn
   b to give advice

3 The study notes that vegetarians had lower overall cholesterol levels than their meat-eating counterparts. It went on to say that, concerning cholesterol types, vegetarians had higher amounts of 'good' cholesterol, or HDL.

   a to elaborate on a fact
   b to give an example

4 I've seen people in restaurants not only order large portions of meat, but also eat only half of what's on their plate. Besides being senseless, I think that's irresponsible.

   a to express an opinion
   b to warn

5 I'm trying to organise a dinner at the new vegetarian restaurant in my neighbourhood. Write back as soon as you can and let me know which is the best night for you.

   a to make a suggestion
   b to make plans

6 This new law will make it legal to sell genetically-modified produce in our supermarkets. We must demand that the law be overturned before it's too late.

   a to warn
   b to explain a step in a process

7 A few of the urban farms in the city are bringing vegetable and herb production right into our neighbourhoods. The one on the corner of Grove Street and Sussex Avenue does exactly that.

   a to give an example
   b to make a suggestion

8 I've often heard people say that they wish they could give up meat, but they just can't seem to make it happen. I say to those people, go to your fridge, throw out all the meat products and don't look back!

   a to make a suggestion
   b to make plans

8 Read the extract from a magazine article. Match the sentences with the functions.

[1] I've been a vegetarian for sixteen years and a vegan for the last six years. [2] Although it's a challenge to maintain the lifestyle, I'm very happy that I've made the decision to do so. [3] In order to maintain a vegan diet, there are a number of things you must look out for – you may think you're buying something that doesn't contain meat or dairy products, but in fact there may be some hidden processed ingredients that do in fact come from animals. [4] The first thing to do is to look carefully at product labels and the various minor ingredients that are listed. [5] If an item contains gelatine, it is neither vegan nor vegetarian, as gelatine is an animal substance, made from the bones of animals. [6] Therefore, this is something you absolutely must avoid, in order to maintain a vegan diet, or a vegetarian one for that matter. [7] If you're truly determined to live a vegan lifestyle, access sources on the internet and visit bookshops or libraries to find lists of vegan foods.

1 ___   **a** to introduce a process   **5** ___   **e** to give background information

2 ___   **b** to give a warning   **6** ___   **f** to give a step in a process

3 ___   **c** to make a suggestion   **7** ___   **g** to provide an example

4 ___   **d** to express a feeling

9 What was the writer's purpose in writing the article in exercise 8?

   a to report   **b** to entertain   **c** to inform   **d** to advertise

Exam focus: understanding purpose and function in *First*

1 Look at the exam practice section on page 44 and read the first paragraph. What is the writer's purpose in writing this paragraph?

  a to discuss how he or she relates to the topic
  b to give an entertaining story about a dinner party
  c to complain about other people's eating habits
  d to define what a typical vegetarian is

2 In the same paragraph, what is the writer's purpose in talking about 'rules'?

  a to inform readers about the rules of vegetarianism
  b to suggest what rules all vegetarians should follow
  c to explain the writer's personal rules of vegetarianism
  d to name the top two rules concerning vegetarianism

3 Read this extract and answer the questions.

> Some vegetarians include tofu in their diet, but what exactly is it? Many people may avoid eating tofu, because they don't have a clue about what it is. It's actually not as strange as it may seem. It's made from soybeans, which are similar to ordinary green beans but have a milder taste. To make tofu, soybeans are crushed with water to make soymilk. The milk is then allowed to sit and eventually the protein in the milk becomes solid. This solid part is removed and pressed to get rid of any extra liquid and the result is a block of tofu. Of course, knowing what tofu is and how it's made might not help you to gain an appreciation of it. In fact, it may make it seem worse. However, many people do love cheese, which is made from cow's milk in exactly the same way.

1 The phrase 'don't have a clue' means people
  A don't want to know something.
  B don't have any information about something.
  C don't need information about something.
  D don't know quite enough about something.

2 Why does the writer mention green beans?
  A to give an example
  B to rephrase an idea
  C to provide a point of reference
  D to state an opinion

3 The description of the tofu-making process
  A helps to make tofu seem less strange.
  B provides a useful set of instructions.
  C shows how difficult it is to make.
  D explains how long it takes to make.

4 Which is NOT a reason the writer mentions cheese?
  A to provide an interesting fact
  B to explain what tofu tastes like
  C to get people to try tofu
  D to compare tofu to a common food

5 What's the purpose of this excerpt?
  A to praise the health benefits of tofu
  B to explain why people hate tofu
  C to teach people how to make tofu
  D to familiarise people with tofu

4 In *First* Paper 1 Part 7, for which question would you need to understand the purpose and function of a text?

  a Which person has only travelled with other people?
  b Which person is expressing an opinion about a lifestyle?

Skills tip

In *First* Paper 1 Part 5, to determine the writer's purpose, it's helpful to

a consider what kind of text the writer wrote.
        Yes / No

b identify the main topic of the text. **Yes / No**

Exam practice:
First Paper 1 Part 5

You are going to read an article about vegetarianism. For questions 1–6, choose the answer (A, B, C or D) which you think fits best according to the text.

GIVING VEGETARIANISM
a chance

I don't consider myself to be a vegetarian, at least not in the strictest sense of the term. The two rules I follow as a semi-vegetarian – if that's even a proper phrase – are that I never cook meals at home using meat, nor do I order meat dishes when dining out. Obviously, these aren't the only occasions when I have meals. My friends sometimes throw dinner parties and I wouldn't want to force my dietary beliefs upon them. So I eat whatever they prepare. If they've spent an hour roasting a leg of lamb or a side of beef, I can make an exception to my diet and tuck in along with the rest of the guests.

Mind you, I'm not offended by the taste of meat at all. On the contrary, I love the worst that meat has to offer – greasy hamburgers, savoury ribs dripping in barbecue sauce and thick, grilled steaks still pink in the middle. As a matter of fact, I grew up eating that kind of food. As an adult, however, I became more conscious of my eating habits. I started to consume less and less meat, until one day I found that I could go for months without eating any meals containing meat at all. I began to explore the idea of giving up animal-based foods altogether, just to see how I would get on.

Soon enough, a whole new world of food opened up to me. I started eating a lot of vegetables and not just ordinary, tasteless salads tossed with a bit of dressing. I would steam broccoli and have it with rice and soy sauce. I would sauté courgettes and aubergines in olive oil and basil. I would try my hand at making vegetable soup with pasta, creamy mushroom soup and spicy cabbage soup (not one of my best creations, I'll admit). What I discovered is that maintaining a vegetarian diet is not only healthy, delicious and inexpensive, it's also abundant in variety. But there was one thing I couldn't quite shake from my mind – why isn't this way of eating more popular?

Even with all the health benefits of a vegetarian diet – lower risk of heart attack, prevention of high blood pressure, reduced rates of cancer – there still seems to be a complete lack of vegetarian eateries and a shortage of vegetarian options at most restaurants. I began to wonder if people were simply addicted to meat. That may be true for some, but for others who might give vegetarianism a try, I realised that there was something else in the way – the culture of vegetarianism appeared to be unpleasant. It seems that there are too many vegetarians who believe that their way of eating is superior to any other. They aren't just vegetarians, they're better people, or so they think. This is rather offensive. You walk into a vegetarian restaurant and suddenly you feel guilty for having eaten that chicken wing at your parents' house the week before. Even someone like me, who eats meat extremely rarely, feels a bit uncomfortable within that whole atmosphere.

So, I propose that we, the vegetarians of the world – again, assuming I can be considered a part of that group, or would even want to be – should become more relaxed about our meat-eating counterparts having a steaming cup of beef stew or sprinkling sliced chicken bits all over their salad, when and if they ever have one. Perhaps, if vegetarianism is seen to be an attractive alternative, more people might try it. It would be a shame for the idea to become trendy, only to go out of fashion in a few years' time. I suppose, for vegetarianism to take root in society for all to enjoy, it needs to change its image to one that is fun, inviting and worth following.

61

1 The writer eats his friends' meals because
  A he feels as though he's got no choice.
  B it doesn't violate any of his rules.
  C he wants to be a polite guest.
  D the taste of meat is appealing.

2 How did the writer give up meat?
  A He did it through a gradual process.
  B He just decided one day to give it up.
  C He set himself a goal of eating no meat.
  D He reverted to the eating habits of his childhood.

3 In the third paragraph, the writer
  A talks about a few badly-prepared meals.
  B discusses the wide selection of vegetarian dishes available.
  C realises why vegetarianism isn't popular.
  D discusses the kinds of dishes he cannot eat.

4 The writer says the main problem with vegetarians is that they are
  A aggressive.
  B arrogant.
  C rude.
  D unsocial.

5 The phrase 'take root' in line 61 refers to vegetarianism becoming more
  A valuable.
  B fashionable.
  C exciting.
  D established.

6 The writer's purpose in writing this article is to
  A argue against the main point of discussion.
  B persuade readers to change habits.
  C provide information about a lifestyle.
  D express opinions and make suggestions.

Skills tip

A good approach to Part 5 is to quickly read the text for gist before attempting to answer the questions. Then, when you get to the questions, you'll have a good idea of where the information is located. You will probably have to re-read portions of the text with extra care in order to pinpoint the answers but, because you've read the entire text, you should know approximately where in the text to look.

6 Understanding cohesion

Green organisations

UNIT AIMS

Skill: understanding cohesion

Vocabulary: environment topic vocabulary

Exam practice: *First* Paper 1 Part 6

Improve your reading skills: understanding cohesion

What is understanding cohesion?

*Cohesion is the way parts of a text are connected to each other. They might be connected by grammar. For example, conjunctions (*and, but, although*), pronouns (*she, they, we*) and articles connect ideas together. Parts of a text might also be connected by synonyms (*e.g.* animal, creature, it*) or by adverbs and phrases (*e.g.* However, On the other hand, Furthermore*). Cohesion is closely related to coherence (Unit 8).*

1 Which of the following does not help cohesion?

 A synonyms

 B capital letters

Why is understanding cohesion important?

Different parts of a sentence are connected to each other. We need to understand how they are connected so that we can understand the meaning of the sentence. In a similar way, different parts of a text are connected. To understand the whole text, we need to understand how the parts are connected. Cohesive devices (all the words and phrases that help create cohesion) tell us about main points, examples, further points, etc, and show us when different sentences are talking about the same thing.

2 If we don't understand cohesion, we can't understand

 A the whole meaning of a text.

 B any of the sentences in a text.

How do you understand cohesion?

*Look out for cohesive devices. This means spotting and understanding connecting phrases and conjunctions. Also, watch out for synonyms and pay attention to grammatical reference words (*this, it, that, *etc). Ask yourself what other things they refer to, either before or after them in the text.*

3 With a word like 'this', you should ask yourself

 A why the writer has used it.

 B what it refers to.

How is understanding cohesion important in *First*?

Understanding cohesion is an important part of all reading, so it's important in First *Paper 1 Parts 5, 6 and 7. In Parts 5 and 7, it helps you to see the way the text is organised so that you can understand the main ideas, supporting examples and other details. In Part 6, understanding cohesion is particularly important because it helps you to see how the removed sentences are connected to different parts of the text.*

4 In *First* Paper 1 Part 6, understanding cohesion is useful because it helps you

 A recreate the original text.

 B understand why a sentence has been removed.

Get started

Look at the photo and answer the questions.

- What environmental problem is represented by the picture?
- What different things can be done to deal with this problem?

Develop your vocabulary

1 Match the words to make phrases.

1	endangered	___	**a**	energy
2	fossil	___	**b**	species
3	renewable	___	**c**	spill
4	oil	___	**d**	layer
5	ozone	___	**e**	fuel

2 Write a word or phrase from the box to complete the text.

crops ■ deforestation ■ extinct ■ habitat ■ mining ■ pesticides ■ set up ■ shortage ■ smog ■ visibility

---

Sign up to *NatureSave!*

Why did a group of local people decide to (**1**) _____ the green organisation *NatureSave*? It was because we realised that people in the area are doing so many things to damage the environment.

One major problem is the widespread cutting down of trees, known as (**2**) _____ . The land is then used to build factories on. These factories produce air pollution, and we now have a major problem in the city with (**3**) _____ , which is a horrible, dirty mixture of smoke and fog. On some days, (**4**) _____ is absolutely terrible.

Another related problem is that a number of animals and insects that lived in the local forests have lost their natural (**5**) _____ and so are becoming (**6**) _____ .

A different problem is that a lot of the land round here that used to be used for growing (**7**) _____ has been sold to companies (**8**) _____ coal. Because of this, we now have a (**9**) _____ of local fresh fruit and vegetables. What's more, the farmers who are still growing produce are now using harmful (**10**) _____ .

So, we've got a lot of work to do to try and educate people. I hope you decide to join us in our struggle!

Develop your reading skills: understanding cohesion

1 Underline the word or phrase in each second sentence that has a similar meaning to the word or phrase in bold.

Example:
 a The **preservation** of the environment is something which we all need to think about.
 b If we <u>protect</u> what we have, then the world will be a safer place for future generations.

1 a Members of this organisation are **dedicated** to saving endangered species from extinction.
 b This commitment is reflected in our many active campaigns both at home and internationally.

2 a Industrialisation has had a terrible **impact** on the quality of the air in our cities.
 b The results can be clearly seen in the statistics regarding premature deaths.

3 a Many people use the argument that we have a duty to save **animals that are under threat**.
 b They claim that it is a disgrace that we do so little for endangered species.

4 a We have nearly used up our resources of **coal, gas and oil**.
 b These so-called fossil fuels have taken billions of years to form.

5 a The **destruction** of the rainforests means that many birds and insects lose their natural habitats.
 b There are fears that the damage may be irreversible and that thousands of species will become extinct.

6 a Our rivers and lakes have been **contaminated** by chemicals from both industry and agriculture.
 b Nobody knows what the long-term effects of this kind of pollution will be.

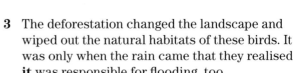

2 Decide what each word in bold refers to.

1 Joining an organisation is likely to be far more effective than simply working alone. **This** is clearly the best way to achieve your goal.
 a joining an organisation
 b working alone
 c achieving your goal

2 **They** are different ages and offer a variety of skills but really make a difference. We must thank the dedicated volunteers who give up their evenings and weekends to help.
 a skills
 b dedicated volunteers
 c evenings and weekends

3 The deforestation changed the landscape and wiped out the natural habitats of these birds. **It** was only when the rain came that they realised **it** was responsible for flooding, too.
 a The deforestation
 b the landscape
 c the rain

4 As **they** gathered for a series of meetings on climate problems, the members' main concern was to set targets on carbon emissions.
 a climate problems
 b targets
 c members

3 Read the paragraph and circle the correct words or phrases.

Throughout history, people have been aware of the environment **(1) but / and**, thousands of years ago, early communities would have had to deal with floods, storms and periods of drought, just as we do today. **(2) As a result / Instead** of such problems, early civilisations had to move elsewhere, or even died out altogether. **(3) Despite / Because of** this, at various points throughout history, tsunamis, hurricanes, earthquakes and volcanic eruptions were occasional violent reminders of the difficulties of living with nature. Climate change is also a natural phenomenon, of course, and we know that ice ages had a huge impact on early populations. **(4) However / Because of this**, we have only recently become aware of the damage that humans are doing to the planet. Most people believe that environmental awareness only began in the last two hundred years. **(5) In fact / For example**, this period really only refers to the realisation that humans are causing the problems.

4 Write a word from the box in each gap to complete the paragraph. There are five words which you do not need to use.

although ■ and ■ but ■ furthermore ■ he
■ however ■ so ■ there ■ this ■ which

People today tend to think of the greenhouse effect as a relatively new phenomenon of the late 20th and early 21st century. **(1)** _____ , before 1900, Swedish scientist Svante Arrhenius found a link between human activity and the balance of nature. In developing his theory to explain the ice ages, **(2)** _____ predicted that the carbon dioxide produced by industry would prevent a new ice age from happening. **(3)** _____ was an early understanding of the phenomenon of global warming. For over 60 years, most scientists believed that Arrhenius was wrong, **(4)** _____ we now know that his theories were very accurate. These days, we all recognise that global warming is a potentially disastrous phenomenon, **(5)** _____ this was not the way Arrhenius saw it. He thought it would save the planet and improve the climate so that we could grow more food for the rising population.

5 Read the short texts and write 'Yes' or 'No' to answer each question.

1 Do NGOs receive money from the government?

_____

Some environmental organisations receive money from the government. On the other hand, NGOs are organisations that generate their own finances.

2 Did the man continue to support most of the organisation's work?

_____

He left the organisation after a disagreement over their nuclear policy, although he remained a supporter of their other campaigns.

3 Did they believe that humans were responsible for climate change?

_____

They accepted that climate change existed but insisted that it was a natural phenomenon.

4 Were environmental organisations in 1900 operating on a global scale?

_____

Several environmental organisations existed in 1900. However, their work was limited to regional or specialised causes such as the setting up of national parks or discouraging women from wearing bird feathers as a fashion statement.

6 Complete the sentences with ideas of your own.

1 Air pollution is a major problem in our cities. Because of this, …
2 We know the environment is in danger so …
3 Farmers use expensive chemicals when growing food. What's more, …
4 Some species of birds are threatened with extinction but …
5 Industries are mainly interested in making money. As a result, …
6 The countryside used to be a completely natural environment. However, …

7 Write one word in each gap to complete the paragraph.

Most of us associate air pollution with cars, factories and power stations. **(1)** _____ , there is at least one case of air pollution that goes back hundreds of years. In 1306, King Edward the First of England banned the burning of a type of fuel called sea coal. It got this name **(2)** _____ it was found and collected on beaches. Sea coal was a great advantage for ordinary people because **(3)** _____ did not need to rely on the primitive mining industry. **(4)** _____ , it was free. At that time, most people used to burn wood to heat their homes **(5)** _____ a sudden shortage of wood meant that people had to find an alternative source of fuel. and sea coal began to be widely used for heating homes. The problem with sea coal is that **(6)** _____ produces much more smoke than wood does. Soon, towns and cities became dirty, smelly and unhealthy and the smog in London was said to be unbearable. **(7)** _____ the King's efforts, the problem was never really solved.

8 Read the text. Decide whether each sentence follows naturally on from the end of the text. Write 'Yes' or 'No'. If you write 'No', explain why not.

Friends of the Earth was founded in 1969 in the United States. It is currently active in 74 countries, protecting the environment and encouraging recycling. The organisation recognises that the Earth is the only home we have, and it is dedicated to taking better care of it. At the heart of many of its campaigns is the idea that rich countries which have exploited poorer countries have a responsibility to do something to repay the debt.

1 Current campaigns include putting pressure on governments to stop climate change. _____

2 This can only be achieved if people learn to respect their own environment. _____

3 In this way, the organisation hopes to stop, or even reverse, the damage that has been done.

Exam focus:
understanding cohesion in *First*

1 Look at the exam practice section on pages 52 and 53 and tick the statements that are true.

Understanding cohesion will help you

1 get a general understanding of the main idea of the text. ___

2 decide which sentence fits in a gap. ___

3 decide which sentences don't fit in a gap. ___

4 decide which sentence doesn't fit in any gap. ___

5 make a guess if you're not 100% sure. ___

6 check your answers at the end. ___

Skills tip

In *First* Paper 1 Part 6, should you look for cohesive devices

a in the missing sentences only?   **Yes / No**

b in the missing sentences and the sentences before and after the gaps?
   Yes / No

2 Read the paragraph and write a sentence to complete the gap.

> People have suggested many points in history as the start of the green movement, but one stands out from all the rest because we have a clear image of it.
>
> _____
>
> It was taken in 1968 by the astronauts on the Apollo 8 mission and was the first colour photo taken of the Earth from a distance. For many, it symbolised how small and fragile the Earth is, and made us realise how important it is for us to look after it.

3 Choose the best sentence to complete the gap in the paragraph in exercise 2.

a Space travel gave us a fantastic opportunity to study what conditions were like on the Moon and how they compared with the Earth.

b The photo, which has become known as *Earthrise*, shows the Earth as a tiny, blue planet, alone in the blackness of space.

c For example, the London smog of 1952, the Bikini Atoll bomb tests of 1954, the book *Silent Spring* in 1962 and the Santa Barbara oil spill of 1969 have all been put forward.

4 Tick the things that helped you choose your answer in exercise 3.
Note down any relevant information.

1 ___ a clear link to the sentence before the gap   _____

2 ___ a clear link to the sentence after the gap   _____

3 ___ cohesive devices such as *he/it/they/this/these/those*   _____

4 ___ cohesive devices such as *and/so/however/also*   _____

5 ___ synonymous words or phrases   _____

5 Which statement is true about *First* Paper 1?

a Understanding cohesion only helps with Part 6.

b Understanding cohesion only helps with Parts 5, 6, and 7.

c Understanding cohesion helps with all the texts in Paper 1.

Exam practice:
First Paper 1 Part 6

You are going to read an article about the history of environmental problems. Six sentences have been removed from the article. Choose from the sentences A–G the one which fits each gap (1–6). There is one extra sentence which you do not need to use.

WAKING UP TO
environmental issues

Jane Logue explains how the race to save the planet gathered speed.

It wasn't until around 200 years ago that we began to become seriously concerned about the negative impact that humans were having on the environment. There were two closely-related reasons for this realisation.

The first of these was that there was a significant rise in the population. Large numbers of people were now polluting our rivers and lakes, and cutting down our trees. **1 [ ]** Manufacturing processes caused people's health to suffer and we became aware of the damage being done to the landscape by activities such as deforestation, mining for coal and steel-making.

We could no longer close our eyes to the facts. There were simply too many people causing too much damage to our planet. Recognising the problem, the United States began creating National Parks. These were large areas of land where development and industry were not allowed. One of the people behind the setting up of the first National Parks was John Muir, an early environmentalist who also became president of the Sierra Club. **2 [ ]**

Still operating today, the Sierra Club is active in many areas, particularly in campaigning to end our dependence on fossil fuels and to explore renewable energy sources such as wind and solar power. **3 [ ]** But although several green organisations existed on both sides of the Atlantic in the first half of the 20th century, their power was limited.

In London in 1952, there was an incident that many say started the environmental movement. A combination of weather conditions and coal smoke led to several days of severe smog in England's capital. The consequences at the time seemed to be confined to traffic problems and cancelled sporting fixtures due to poor visibility. However, it soon became clear that thousands of people had died as a direct result of the air pollution in that short period of time. **4 [ ]**

Since the 1950s, however, our planet has had to face a range of new threats. For example, the widespread use of pesticides in the US inspired a book by Rachel Carson in 1962 called *Silent Spring*, which became a bestseller. **5 [ ]**

Meanwhile, the World Wildlife Fund (WWF) was established to protect the habitats of wild animals and stop endangered species from becoming extinct. The development of nuclear weapons and nuclear power led to the forming of groups such as Greenpeace, and a series of well-documented oil spills helped draw attention to the environmental catastrophes that humankind was capable of bringing about. **6 [ ]** Acid rain, the hole in the ozone layer and genetically modified crops have given rise to a vast number of organisations dedicated to limiting the damage. But, even with thousands of green organisations in the UK alone, it's tempting to wonder whether the race to secure a better future is one that we are winning.

A In the UK, it wasn't until the 1950s that the first National Park was set up.

B Today, we have no shortage of environmental concerns, or of groups committed to dealing with them.

C The other key factor was the rise of industry.

D Here too, the Americans were far behind the rest of the world.

E The popularity of this publication showed just how many people were against interfering with the natural balance of nature.

F This was founded in 1892 and was one of the first environmental organisations in the United States.

G The city was forced to face up to its problems, and action was taken to make sure such a tragedy would not happen again.

Skills tip

When you do *First* Paper 1 Part 6, remember that the missing sentence could link to the sentence before the gap, the sentence after the gap, or both. In some cases, the link is not in the sentence *immediately* before/after the gap, but one or two sentences earlier or later, so make sure you have a good understanding of the whole text (see Unit 2, reading for gist).

When you're considering a sentence to put in a gap, check to see if there are links to the information before and after that gap. Look for clues such as *they/this/these/those, however/despite, and/also*, synonymous words/phrases, names, dates and ideas that have or haven't already been mentioned.

7

Understanding
attitude and opinion

Traditions around the world

Improve your reading skills: understanding attitude and opinion

What is understanding attitude and opinion?

A writer's attitude and opinion are part of what the writer thinks about a subject. For example, a writer's attitude towards what he or she is writing about could be that it is unacceptable, or that it should happen more. Understanding attitude and opinion involves recognising what is a neutral fact and what is an opinion.

1 Part of understanding attitude and opinion involves
A knowing your own opinions.
B separating fact from opinion.

Why is understanding attitude and opinion important?

Many pieces of writing are a mixture of fact and opinion and you need to be able to separate one from the other. If you don't understand when a writer is giving you their opinion and when they are presenting facts, you cannot properly understand the argument they are making. You are also in danger of accepting as fact things which are actually just the writer's opinion.

2 If you don't recognise when a writer is giving their opinion, you might
A take their opinion as fact.
B miss important facts.

How do you understand attitude and opinion?

Look at ways in which opinions are often expressed. This includes simple phrases like 'I think that ...', but also more complicated forms of expression, such as 'There seems no doubt that ...'. Also look at the precise words a writer chooses. For example, if a writer describes a person as 'thin', 'slim' or 'skinny', we know that the person isn't fat and we can also tell whether the writer sees this as a neutral fact, a positive aspect or a negative aspect.

3 One thing you need to consider is the writer's
A personality.
B choice of words.

How is understanding attitude and opinion important in *First*?

In First *Paper 1 Part 5, you may be asked specific questions about the writer's attitude and opinion on a subject. To answer those questions, it's important that you are able to find and understand points in the text where the writer gives his or her opinion. In Part 6, attitude and opinion are part of the global meaning of a text and understanding that helps you put the removed sentences in the correct gaps. In Part 7, you may be asked to match words or phrases based specifically on the attitudes and opinions you read in the texts.*

4 Specific questions about attitude and opinion may appear in
A Part 5.
B Part 6.

Get started

Look at the photo and answer the questions.

- How common are traditional cultural events in your country?
- Do you think it is important for them to be preserved? Why?/Why not?
- Do you ever attend such events? Why?/Why not?

Develop your vocabulary

1 Choose the correct word to complete the sentences.

1 Ours is a culture _____ in tradition.
   a soaked   **b** steeped

2 My uncle uses a small sharp knife to make _____ out of wood.
   a carvings   **b** carpets

3 Many ancient peoples participated in rituals designed to bring them a good _____ , so that there would be plenty of food to eat throughout the year.
   a heritage   **b** harvest

4 It's not always easy to pin down what national _____ is.
   a personality   **b** identity

5 While I was on holiday in India, I visited the Golden _____ in Amritsar – it is a centre of worship for people of the Sikh religion.
   a Temple   **b** civilisation

2 Write a word or phrase from the box in each gap to complete the text.

customs ▪ die out ▪ rituals ▪ roots ▪ values

Culture is built on the **(1)** _____ and traditions that develop over a long period of time within a particular country or society. The way of life and social organisation of a group of people develop from a set of shared **(2)** _____ and beliefs that influence how people think and behave. Although different cultures have different **(3)** _____ or origins, many share similar **(4)** _____ to celebrate major life events such as birth, death or marriage. With the advent of the modern technology-based society, many traditional cultures have started to **(5)** _____ because of a trend towards globalisation.

3 Match the words with their definitions.

1 heritage   ___
2 community   ___
3 cuisine   ___
4 civilisation   ___
5 ancestor   ___

a the local area where you live, including the people
b a person from whom you are descended
c a society of a particular time and place
d something passed down from previous generations
e the food of a particular country or region

Unit 7

Develop your reading skills: Understanding attitude and opinion

1 Read the text. Which of the statements which follow express opinions and which ones offer facts? Write 'O' for opinion or 'F' for fact.

> Civilisations around the world have produced art dating back to the earliest period of their history. To my mind, there can be no argument that this is proof that art is an essential part of being human. Even before the invention of writing, ancient peoples were producing works of art to express their feelings and to describe their everyday rituals and pastimes. It is wrong to consider this art as primitive. The delicate lines of cave drawings and intricately carved figures from pre-history should be appreciated as products of artists every bit as sophisticated as the ones of the modern world. It is a shame that most people seem to view ancient traditional art forms as basic and simple. You only have to look at the aboriginal art that is still created today to see the skill that is required to combine elegant lines and eye-catching colours in such an expressive way.

1 Creating art has always been a feature of all societies. ____

2 It is part of human nature to create art. ____

3 Before the invention of writing, art was one way that people could express themselves. ____

4 Ancient artists were as skilful as the artists of today. ____

5 Few people appreciate ancient art. ____

6 There isn't much difference between how aboriginal art is produced now and in the past. ____

2 Read the text and answer the questions.

> As a big opera fan, I often ask myself if this art form is actually a part of the culture and traditions of this country or just an old-fashioned form of entertainment for snobs. I suppose there is some truth in that idea but it's not the whole truth. I would suggest that it is still an integral part of our cultural life. However, I'm not sure that it is a medium which is accessible to everyone. Opera as an art form will become irrelevant in our modern society if the opera companies don't do more to attract the interest of people from all backgrounds, in particular the younger generation. As far as I'm concerned, there is a lot we can do to encourage greater participation in the arts. Opera should be for everyone, not just for an elite few. Education has a major role to play but so do the artists themselves. It's my view that the opera community has not done enough to encourage greater public support and interest. It's high time that this changed.

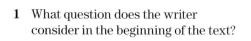

1 What question does the writer consider in the beginning of the text?

_____

2 How does the writer feel about the idea that opera is old-fashioned?

_____

3 What negative opinion does the writer express about the accessibility of opera?

_____

4 Is the writer optimistic about the possibility of making opera more accessible?

_____

5 What two factors does the writer identify as necessary for more people to enjoy opera?

_____

6 What criticism does the writer make about people in the world of opera?

_____

3 Tick the phrases which can be used for introducing an opinion.

1 As far as I'm concerned ... ____
2 I'm not sure that ... ____
3 Personally, I think ... ____
4 I suppose / reckon / guess that I ... ____
5 In spite of being ... ____
6 In my experience ... ____
7 I wonder why ... ____
8 On the contrary ... ____
9 I would suggest that ... ____

4 Using the phrases you ticked in exercise 3, write sentences of your own to answer the questions.

1 Can you learn a lot about the culture and traditions of another country as a tourist?

2 What aspects of your culture can express your national identity?

3 Do you think traditional cultures can survive in the modern world?

4 Should modern societies make an effort to preserve local traditions?

5 Read the pairs of sentences and decide which ones express a personal opinion and which ones express a general opinion. Write 'G' for general or 'P' for personal.

1 a Some people say that technology will destroy traditional customs. ____
   b Personally speaking, I think that other factors are more important in destroying traditions. ____

2 a I would suggest that culture and local customs give people a sense of community. ____
   b It is thought that strong traditions reinforce national identity. ____

3 a It is generally accepted that folk music still has strong roots in local culture. ____
   b In my experience, music is one of the most distinctive aspects of traditional cultures. ____

4 a As far as I'm concerned, not all traditional customs are necessarily a good thing. ____
   b It is considered vital that we preserve our local customs at all costs. ____

6 Choose the correct answer.

1 General opinion is used to show
   a views that are held by most people.
   b only what the writer thinks.

2 A writer may express a general opinion
   a because he or she doesn't have a personal opinion.
   b to contrast with or reinforce his or her own opinion.

7 Read the paragraph and circle the correct words.

> This holiday was a welcome break from my (**1**) **hugely / slightly** stressful life in the city. As soon as I arrived, I felt as if I had entered another world. For one thing, the people of the island are so (**2**) **lazy / relaxed** that no-one ever does anything in a hurry. It was quite refreshing to be able to take my time about life for once. Another aspect of the island which I found wonderful was the traditional local food. The restaurants use only home-grown produce which is cooked (**3**) **perfectly / quite well**. Perhaps I enjoyed it a bit too much as I came home a little (**4**) **overweight / obese**. But it was a small price to pay for such a (**5**) **reasonable / pleasant** stay amongst such hospitable people.

8 Which of the sentences a or b has the same meaning as the first sentence?

1 The women of the village wear extraordinarily beautiful jewellery.

    a I thought the jewellery the women in the village wore was quite pretty.   ___

    b The jewellery the women in the village wore was absolutely gorgeous.   ___

2 I couldn't begin to describe how deafening the tribal drums were.

    a I don't want to describe how loud the tribal drums were.   ___

    b It's very difficult to describe how loud the tribal drums were.   ___

3 It seems to me that some tourists think local traditions are simply a form of entertainment.

    a I agree that local traditions should be regarded as entertainment for visitors.   ___

    b I don't think tourists should just see local traditions as something to entertain them.   ___

4 The destruction of the local culture has had a devastating effect on the community.

    a The destruction of the local culture has had a huge impact on the people in the community.   ___

    b The destruction of the local culture has had a limited effect on the community.   ___

5 I guess that most people would enjoy the folk music of this region.

    a I'm certain that most people would enjoy the folk music of this region.   ___

    b I suppose that most people would enjoy the folk music of this region.   ___

9 Choose the best sentence to fill each gap. There is one extra sentence you do not need to use.

Protecting traditional cultures is by no means an easy task. The task isn't helped by the fact that opinion is divided amongst the various experts on how to go about it. **(1)** ___ These can include lack of employment in rural areas, the effects of war or drought and the advancement of technology in traditional societies. Many of these problems can be very difficult to control. **(2)** ___ Is it possible, or even desirable, to sustain traditional cultures artificially? For example, we cannot insist that remote settlements use their traditional forms of communication rather than mobile phones. **(3)** ___ This would not benefit anyone, least of all the traditional cultures themselves. It seems to me that the best approach is firstly to record as much as we can about traditional cultures. **(4)** ___

a One result of such a strategy is that such areas become more like a theme park for tourists than a real community in which people live and work.

b In my view, we should examine the reasons why so many traditional societies are close to collapse.

c Then we can try to create conditions that encourage their continued existence.

d It is doubtful whether they will ever agree.

e But another question worth asking is, even if we could, should we?

Exam focus:
understanding
attitude and opinion in *First*

1 Look at the exam practice section on pages 60 and 61 and answer the questions.

  1 What are the texts about according to the title and subtitle?
    a the way of life in different places   **b** the benefits of modern society

  2 How many times can you choose the different people (A–D) in your answers?
    a only once   **b** more than once

  3 Is it a good idea to underline the key words in the questions?
    a Yes, it is.   **b** No, it isn't.

2 Tick the ideas that are good techniques for *First* Paper 1, Part 7.

  1 Scan the texts for words that are synonyms of words in the questions. ___

  2 Read all the texts slowly several times before reading the questions. ___

  3 Look out for phrases in the text that show opinion and attitude. ___

  4 Once you identify a part of a text related to a question, read it carefully. ___

  5 Answer questions quickly as you won't have time to check them. ___

3 Read the pairs of sentences and decide which ones are opinions.

  1 **a** Unfortunately, our society appears to be changing very rapidly.
      b Less than 30% of the population are involved in traditional craftwork.

  2 **a** The city is well-known for the number of cultural events that take place there.
      b The loss of funding for the festival is a shameful development.

  3 **a** Most people agree that it's important to keep traditions alive.
      b The government recognises the rights of native peoples.

  4 **a** Schools should do more to help preserve regional languages.
      b The school runs a language course for students on Saturdays.

4 Look again at the sentences you chose in exercise 3 and underline examples of these things.

  1 a qualifying adjective
  2 an indirect expression of opinion (*there seems no doubt that ... etc*)
  3 a modal verb
  4 a qualifying adverb

> **Skills tip**
>
> In *First* Paper 1 Part 7, attitude and opinion
>
> a can be found in the texts only. **Yes / No**
> b are always used in all the questions. **Yes / No**
> c can be found in both the questions and texts. **Yes / No**

5 Decide if the statements are true (T) or false (F).

  1 Opinion and attitude are only expressed with phrases such as: *I think, I believe, In my opinion* etc. ___

  2 Understanding attitude and opinion is only useful for Part 7 of Paper 1. ___

  3 Understanding attitude and opinion is useful for Parts 5, 6 and 7 of Paper 1. ___

  4 Being able to tell the difference between fact and opinion is a useful skill for analysing texts. ___

Exam practice:
First Paper 1 Part 7

You are going to read an article where people describe the traditions and customs of their country. For questions 1–10, choose from the people (A–D). The people may be chosen more than once.

Which person

explains how today's cultural activities are influenced by their ancestors?	**1**
thinks that prosperity has affected traditions and beliefs in their society?	**2**
compares the small size of their country with its influence on the surrounding region?	**3**
describes how a traditional custom is related to people's beliefs about food?	**4**
contrasts their country's difficult past with its varied cultural heritage?	**5**
says that one of their traditions has roots in both ancient and modern religion?	**6**
explains how a traditional event got its name?	**7**
mentions the prestige associated with a particular cultural event?	**8**
emphasises how a cultural event brings the people of the country together?	**9**
explains how other nations have influenced all aspects of their culture?	**10**

Skills tip

The ability to tell the difference between facts and opinions is a skill that will help in many parts of *First* Paper 1. It will help you to identify the type of information you need to find in texts. To identify what parts of a text offer an opinion, look for words and phrases such as *I think/feel/believe, As far as I'm concerned, Most people agree that,* as well as qualifying adjectives and adverbs and modal verbs expressing what people *could/should/must* do.

KEEPING TRADITION *Alive*

Four people discuss the culture of their countries

A Jussi Koskinen – Finland

The Republic of Finland is a country steeped in tradition. Although we are one of the smaller north European countries, we have probably made a larger contribution to Europe's cultural traditions than our geographically larger neighbours. We have a strong sense of national identity, rooted in our country's history and cultural heritage. Many of our holidays and celebrations are a mixture of the 1,000-year old Christian influence and the remains of old Finnish pagan traditions. My favourite celebration of the year is Juhannus, when we celebrate the summer solstice by lighting a huge bonfire. Before 1316 this was a pagan festival known as Ukon juhla, but it was subsequently renamed Juhannus after John the Baptist. In ancient folklore, midsummer was a night of powerful magic when fairies were believed to appear. What makes this night even more special is Finland's famous 'midnight sun' – around midsummer the sun never sets and the night is little more than a darkening of the sky.

B Farisha Da Silva – Trinidad and Tobago

Unlike some parts of the Caribbean, the Republic of Trinidad and Tobago has a strong and growing economy due to its petroleum industry – our country is the leading Caribbean producer of oil and gas. The downside of this, it seems to me, is that, as the country has become wealthier, many of our customs and even our values have changed. That said, two things unite everyone in this country – calypso and carnival. Calypso is a style of music which originated here around the beginning of the 20th century and has its roots in West African music. The annual Trinidad and Tobago carnival is the most significant event on the islands' cultural and tourism calendar. Carnival time is definitely my favourite time of year. The parades are fantastic and the steel bands get everyone dancing in the streets. Today musical competitions make up a large part of the carnival – every musician on the islands fights for the honour of being named 'Calypso Monarch' and the competition is broadcast live on TV.

C Arus Magapian – Armenia

Armenia is a country with a long and troubled history and war and bloodshed have characterised our recent past. The country has also suffered economically and today poverty and unemployment are very high. Armenia is a poor country but it is rich in tradition. Due to its geographical position on the old caravan routes at the crossroads between Europe, Asia and the Middle East, Armenian culture has been influenced by many different societies and civilisations. Greek, Persian, Turkish and Arab influences can be seen in our cuisine, our folk dancing and music and our beautiful, bright traditional costumes. Undoubtedly, the tradition that Armenia is best known for is carpet weaving. For hundreds of years, women have been the main weavers. Each carpet is a work of art and the symbols and designs used are like a 'text' that tells the story of Armenian beliefs and rituals. The carpets and other woven textiles are used to cover floors, walls and furniture and are often, but not always, in deep, dark red colours.

D Wayan Balik – Bali

Balinese culture is a combination of religion, tradition and art. In our country, we consider religion to be art and most people are enthusiastic artists. We spend a lot of our free time using the skills which have been passed down to us from our parents' and grandparents' generations to create works of art. These artworks can take the form of beautiful paintings, extraordinary carvings, superb weaving, and even rice decorations that are displayed in public temples or in homes. Nowhere is this artistic expression better displayed than at the annual Bali Kite Festival. The kites are believed to send a message to the gods asking for a good harvest. Traditional giant kites are made and flown by teams from local villages. The beautiful kites include fish, bird and leaf shapes and red, white and black are traditional colours used in the kites' design. Sometimes the kites lose height and fall down into the water-logged rice fields – then it's a race through the water to rescue the kite. Great fun!

8

Understanding coherence

Healthcare and health systems

UNIT AIMS

Skill: understanding coherence

Vocabulary: health and fitness topic vocabulary

Exam practice: *First* Paper 1 Part 6

Improve your reading skills: understanding coherence

What is understanding coherence?

Understanding coherence means understanding the logical meaning of a text. In narrative texts, such as stories or biographical texts, it includes following the logical order of events. In argumentative texts, such as articles and essays, it includes following the writer's logic and the way the argument is put together. Coherence is closely related to cohesion (Unit 6).

1 Part of understanding coherence in a story is

    A understanding what characters think.

    B knowing in what order things happened.

Why is understanding coherence important?

Understanding coherence is part of understanding the global meaning of a text. If you don't understand the way the ideas in a text work together, you can't fully understand the text. You will get confused about the order of events or about the argument a writer is presenting. You need to understand the function of different parts of a text, in order to decide whether you agree or disagree with the writer and why.

2 Understanding coherence will help you

    A come up with new ideas on the topic of the text.

    B form your own opinion of what the writer is saying.

How do you understand coherence?

Part of understanding coherence is understanding cohesion (unit 6). It also involves considering how a text is organised, how ideas are connected and how they relate to the topic. You use clues in the text as well as your own knowledge to do this.

3 One important part of coherence is to think about

    A logical connections between ideas.

    B punctuation.

How is understanding coherence important in *First*?

Understanding coherence is particularly important in First *Paper 1 Parts 5 and 6. In Part 5, you may be asked questions about the logic of the text or the way it is organised. In Part 6, understanding coherence helps you to work out the relationship between different parts of the text to put the removed sentences back in the correct place.*

4 In *First* Paper 1 Part 5, you could be asked

    A about the structure of the text.

    B to explain what coherence is.

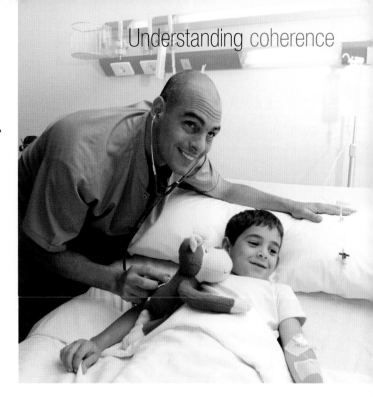

Get started

Look at the photo and answer the questions.

- What job is this person doing?
  Would you like to do this job? Why?/Why not?
- What might be difficult about this job?
  Choose from the list.

> boredom ■ emotional pain ■ long hours ■ paperwork ■ stress

- What might be rewarding about the job?
  Choose from the list.

> helping people ■ interesting work ■ long holidays ■ pay ■ variety

Develop your vocabulary

1 Match the words with their definitions.

1 ward	____	**a** something that is put on the skin to kill bacteria
2 patient	____	**b** somebody who a doctor is trying to cure
3 infection	____	**c** a room in a hospital with many beds
4 bedridden	____	**d** forced to stay in bed due to illness
5 antiseptic	____	**e** a disease caused by bacteria entering the body
6 treatment	____	**f** the method a doctor uses to cure somebody

2 Complete each sentence using a word from the box.

> bedside ■ life ■ mortality ■ natural ■ nurse ■ public

1 The old man died of _____ **causes** at the age of 95.

2 In the interests of _____ **health**, no-one can leave the town where the epidemic has broken out.

3 The doctor had a wonderful _____ **manner** and made patients feel secure.

4 The _____ **rate** among children in the developing world is still too high.

5 _____ **expectancy** in 19th century hospitals was extremely low – hundreds of patients died of infection due to poor sanitary conditions.

6 After years of working on the wards, she has been promoted to **head** _____.

3 Read the paragraph and circle the correct words.

To: All nurses

From: The head nurse

Please remember that while you are (**1**) **on / at** duty, you are responsible for the medical care and well-being of the patients. Make sure they are checked (**2**) **in / on** every 30 minutes at least (more often in critical cases), and that any patient who is (**3**) **in / of** pain is given pain relief as soon as possible. We have people suffering (**4**) **of / from** some very serious diseases on this ward, who need to be looked (**5**) **for / after** properly. If in doubt, call a doctor. Finally, if a patient does pass (**6**) **along / away**, please inform the head nurse and duty doctor immediately.

63

Develop your reading skills: understanding coherence

1 Complete each sentence using a word or phrase from the text.

> Many of the new fitness crazes are high-energy group activities. They tend to push you to your limits and beyond through a combination of trainer enthusiasm and peer pressure. Those people who are just starting such an exercise should be aware of this. It is easy to end up with an injury such as a pulled muscle or even a trip to hospital which may put beginners back on the couch for days, weeks or months.

1 The writer believes that _____ should not do high-energy fitness activities.

2 One minor injury they could suffer from is a(n) _____.

3 This could happen because the group will _____ them to do more than they should.

4 They might be unable to do any _____ for some time because of this.

2 Read the first sentence. Tick the sentence a or b which would follow if a person agreed with the idea in the first sentence.

1 *Surveys have consistently shown that the British public wants a national health service.*

   a Perhaps it's time for politicians to start listening to them. ____

   b Do people always know what's good for them, however? ____

2 *Whenever there are problems in a hospital, the nurses are held responsible.*

   a The newspapers never say anything about cuts and shortages. ____

   b That's because they are on the front line, in direct contact with patients. ____

3 *An annual check-up is said by doctors to be vital for the over-forties.*

   a Some men should consider taking aspirin to prevent heart attacks. ____

   b Even if a patient is in good health, his or her doctor can check for possible future problems. ____

4 *More and more hospitals are being designed as 'patient-focused' care centres.*

   a The needs and wants of the patient and their family should be central to hospital policy. ____

   b Going to hospital can be a frightening and confusing experience. ____

3 Put the sentences into the correct order.

1 ____

2 ____

3 ____

4 ____

5 ____

   a After all, this is the professional who will have access to the entire family in a way that no other specialist will.

   b He or she might also see a number of generations, from grandmother to mother to daughter, for example.

   c A GP or General Practitioner is what the Americans call a 'family doctor', and to my mind the American term is more apt.

   d Having access to patients over a wide age range can help in understanding the causes of illness, including both environmental factors and inherited diseases.

   e He or she might, for example, come to your home to see a sick child.

4 Read the text and number the events in the order they happened.

Until the health scare, Owen had hardly thought about illness, going to his doctor just once in the three years before the scare. He'd always been fit and had even run a marathon once in his twenties. But then, two months before his 40th birthday, he had what the doctor at the hospital later termed a 'mild heart attack'. He was working very hard at the time and had just started a new job, in fact. One day, as he was going out of the door, he felt a sharp pain in his chest.

1 ___   **a** Owen started a new job.
2 ___   **b** Owen ran a marathon.
3 ___   **c** Owen went to his doctor.
4 ___   **d** Owen went to the hospital.
5 ___   **e** Owen had a heart attack.

5 Put the verbs in brackets into the correct form to complete the text.

Just as Dr Slocum (1) _____ (**enter**) the doors of the hospital, an ambulance came driving through the gates, siren blaring and lights flashing. She (2) _____ (**graduate**) from medical school only a few months before, but all that theory (3) _____ (**not prepare**) her for the real thing. '(4) _____ (**you take**) this one, please, Dr Slocum?' said her mentor, Dr Barton, and suddenly she (5) _____ (**stand**) by the back of the ambulance waiting for the doors to open. She (6) _____ (**had**) neither breakfast nor a cup of coffee. The paramedic opened the doors from the inside of the ambulance and (7) _____ (**jump**) out, pulling a stretcher after him. 'There (8) _____ (**be**) a terrible accident on the motorway,' he said. 'There are more on the way.'

6 Write a word from the box in each gap to complete the text. There are three extra words which you do not need to use.

finally ■ firstly ■ lastly ■ meanwhile ■ next ■ other ■ previously ■ then

Dr Maurice Porter may not have won worldwide fame but to the people of this village he was part of the architecture. He had actually been born here, his parents having moved to Wood Green three years (1) _____. His father was a doctor too, so it was natural for him to study medicine. He went abroad to specialise but (2) _____ his father was growing ill. Dr Porter returned home and (3) _____, when it was clear his father would not recover, he gave up his studies. The very (4) _____ day his father's practice was open for business again. When Dr Maurice Porter (5) _____ passed away last week, he had been our village doctor for nearly 50 years.

7 Match the notes with the paragraphs to make a plan for a biographical text.

1 Introduction: ___

2 Paragraph 1: ___

3 Paragraph 2: ___

4 Paragraph 3: ___

5 Conclusion: ___

a birth and early years

b why the subject is important

c death and the subject's further influence

d the subject's first contact with his life's work

e the subject's major achievements

8 Read the introduction to a text and choose the best answers.

> It is perhaps ironic that the success of our public health system is the very thing that is threatening its existence. People are living longer and that means they will need more years of care, something that costs more than our health providers are receiving from health insurance funds. To solve this problem we need to radically rethink our approach to healthcare.

1 What kind of text is this an introduction to?
 a a biography
 b an article
 c a story

2 What is the writer going to talk about?
 a the history of the public health system
 b the end of the public health system
 c a way to save the public health system

9 Read the two paragraphs which follow the text in exercise 8 and answer the questions below.

> The answer is to go to the other end of the age scale: youth. What we must begin to do is to educate our young people on how to live a healthier lifestyle. This would mean, for example, having lessons in school on the dangers of smoking and drinking and on how to eat a balanced diet. **(1)** ___
> What would the result be? A healthier population in general and fewer visits to doctors and hospitals. **(2)** ___ The only way to save our health system is to require it less, which means making an effort to become healthier people for life. The added benefit of having an improved quality of life is also not one to be taken lightly.

1 What would you expect the missing sentence in the first paragraph to be?
 a a rephrasing of the main idea of the paragraph
 b another example of how to make young people healthier
 c an explanation of what the result of the main idea would be

2 What would you expect the missing sentence in the second paragraph to be?
 a another result of the action suggested in the first paragraph
 b a possible danger of the action suggested in the first paragraph
 c an area that would not be affected by the action suggested in the first paragraph

10 Choose the best two sentences to fill the gaps in the text in exercise 9.

a In later life, the aged would be more active, more independent and less likely to need long-term treatment for conditions such as high blood pressure or angina.

b We must, however, be careful not to do too much too soon, since things cannot be undone so easily.

c Teaching our young people how to live in a healthier manner is the one and only solution to this increasingly pressing problem.

d An emphasis on fitness and the importance of physical activity would also be beneficial.

Exam focus:
Understanding coherence in *First*

1 Look at the exam practice section on pages 68 and 69 and tick the ideas you think will help you understand the coherence of the text.

1 Reading the first paragraph carefully. ___

2 Understanding the meaning of difficult words. ___

3 Understanding the purpose of the text. ___

4 Noting the main idea of each paragraph. ___

5 Imagining what the subject of the text looked like. ___

6 Understanding how the writer feels about the subject of the text. ___

Skills tip

In *First* Paper 1 Part 6, you should

a read the paragraphs first and imagine what could be missing. **Yes / No**

b read the missing sentences first and imagine what paragraphs they could fit in. **Yes / No**

2 Choose the best sentence to fill the gap in the text.

The modern craze for vitamins is a consequence of our unhealthy lifestyle. We know we are doing too much too quickly but cannot or will not change our way of life. _____ That takes time however: time to plan a weekly menu, time to shop more than once a week, time to cook. We would rather rush home, grabbing a takeaway on the way – and pop a vitamin pill.

a We have things to do, places to go, that great new action adventure film to see.

b Following a balanced diet with plenty of fresh fruit and vegetables would give us all the vitamins we need.

c Additionally, a vitamin pill is the perfect solution to the problem and swallowing one takes less than a second.

3 How did you choose the correct answer in exercise 2? Match the reasons below with the options in exercise 2. You will use some options more than once.

1 This option fits with the sentence before the gap but not the one after. ___

2 The sentence after the gap explains how to do what is described in this option. ___

3 This option does not fit with how the writer feels about vitamins. ___

4 This option is a bit too positive, considering the tone of the piece. ___

5 There is no first point for this option to add to. ___

4 Decide if the statements are true (T) or false (F).

1 Understanding coherence only helps with *First* Paper 1 Part 6. ___

2 Understanding coherence helps with detail questions in *First* Paper 1 Part 5. ___

3 Understanding coherence helps with sequence questions in *First* Paper 1 Part 5. ___

4 Understanding coherence helps with purpose questions in *First* Paper 1 Part 5. ___

Exam practice:
First Paper 1 Part 6

You are going to read an article about Florence Nightingale, an important figure in nursing. Six sentences have been removed from the article. Choose from the sentences A–G the one which fits each gap (1–6). There is one extra sentence which you do not need to use.

THE LADY WITH
the lamp

Separating the myth of Florence Nightingale from the facts.

The legend of Florence Nightingale, 'the lady with the lamp', conjures up the image of the caring nurse on duty at night, going from ward to ward checking on wounded soldiers in the Crimea. There is no doubt that Nightingale did bring comfort to those men but her success in raising their life expectancy is exaggerated and her real achievements neglected. Following the war and after her return to Britain, she became a well-known health reformer, publishing works on childbirth, public healthcare and hospitals and the treatment of wounded soldiers.

Florence Nightingale was born into a wealthy family and was lucky enough to have a father who believed that women should be educated. This, for him, did not mean simply in the classics, music and painting, which was the limit for even the most accomplished women of the day. **1** The last of these proved especially helpful to her later work in the field of medical statistics.

Her work during the Crimean War was legendary even then, though many improvements made at that time were not her doing. She was not a promoter of antiseptics, for example, since understanding of infection was still basic at that time. However, she did believe people in bad health needed rest and a good diet in order to give their bodies the best chance of recovery. She also used her growing fame to great effect. **2**

She used her public reputation on her return to Britain to set up the Nightingale Training School for nurses. Up to that point, nursing had been under the control of the church: nurses were either nuns or they were trained by nuns. Nightingale's school was the first that was independent of the church and her book, *Notes on Nursing*, published in 1859, carefully emphasised the fact that a nurse practised a profession just as much as a doctor did. **3**

What was perhaps the most interesting aspect of the book was the importance she placed on 'bedside manner' and how to treat bedridden patients in hospital. Doctors came in for some pointed criticism for their failings in this area and nurses were encouraged to make the patients' well-being, physical, mental and emotional, their mission. **4** By 1882, a number of graduates were head nurses at some of the largest hospitals in the country.

She lobbied the British government again in 1858 and 1859 to look into healthcare for the British army in India. She believed the lack of medical care and the poor sanitary conditions were contributing to the high mortality rates amongst army personnel serving in that country. A comprehensive report was prepared and her careful and clear presentation of data made her arguments hard to ignore. After ten years of reform, there was already a massive improvement. **5**

In later life, Florence Nightingale suffered from a disease called brucellosis and, as a result, was often bedridden herself. **6** Her expertise in field medicine was sought after by the Union government during the American Civil War and in 1883 she was awarded the Royal Red Cross by Queen Victoria. She died of natural causes in 1910 at the age of 90, passing away in her sleep. Her personality, work and theories still influence nursing to this day.

A The first nurses who trained at the Nightingale School started working in 1865.

B Nightingale received a well-rounded education which included science, history, philosophy and mathematics.

C This was something that, as a nurse, Nightingale had witnessed first-hand.

D It is still in print – and studied – today.

E Despite often being in great pain, she never tired and she carried out some of her most pioneering work in hospital planning from her bed.

F For example, deaths among soldiers had fallen to 18 per 1,000 from an original rate of 69.

G It was through her efforts that the British government commissioned the engineer Isambard Brunel to design a field hospital.

Skills tip

When you do *First* Paper 1 Part 6, use every clue that is given to you. For example, the title, sub-heading and first paragraph all summarise the text in different ways and at different lengths. Consider these questions: Why has the writer written this text? How does he/she feel about the subject? What main points will be mentioned? This careful reading of the title, sub-heading and first paragraph will help you as you go through the rest of the text. Don't just skip them because there is no missing sentence there. It's the only part of the text that is complete – and that is extremely useful.

9

Understanding exemplification

Fame and celebrity

UNIT AIMS

Skill: understanding exemplification

Vocabulary: people topic vocabulary

Exam practice: *First* Paper 1 Part 5

Improve your reading skills: understanding exemplification

What is understanding exemplification?	*Examples are used in many texts. They are important in supporting and explaining what the writer is saying. Writers use them to show how a general point applies to particular situations. Understanding exemplification means recognising an example when you read it and knowing what it is an example of.*

1 Writers use examples to

   A support the points they are making.

   B avoid providing too much explanation.

Why is understanding exemplification important?	*Writers use examples to support the points they make. When you can recognise and understand the examples, you can judge how successful an argument is. You can judge whether the examples are used correctly and whether you agree with the writer. You can tell if the general points the writer makes apply to specific situations.*

2 Understanding exemplification helps in

   A choosing specific texts to read.

   B judging the success of an argument.

How do you understand exemplification?	*You need to know how writers show that something is an example. This includes simple phrases (for example, for instance, such as) as well as more complicated expressions (This can be seen in ... , One application of this is ...). You also need to recognise examples that are not clearly indicated by phrases and expressions.*

3 You need to

   A focus mostly on complicated example expressions.

   B focus on examples however they are presented.

How is understanding exemplification important in *First*?	*In* First *Paper 1 Part 5, you may be asked questions about how a text is organised, including questions about examples. In* First *Paper 1 Part 6, examples are one of the ways in which different parts of the text are connected. In Part 7, you may need to understand specific details of examples.*

4 Understanding exemplification helps in Part 6 because

   A examples sometimes link parts of the text together.

   B all the removed sentences are usually examples.

Get started

Look at the photo and answer the questions.

- What qualities does a person need in order to be famous?
- What do you believe is more important – being famous or having money? Why?
- What skills and talents must you possess in order to be a famous …
  actor? artist? dancer? scientist? singer? writer?

Develop your vocabulary

1 Match the words with their definitions.

1	appreciative	___	**a**	small light brown spots on your skin
2	confident	___	**b**	friendly
3	dyed	___	**c**	being a little overweight
4	freckles	___	**d**	thankful
5	harsh	___	**e**	shy
6	pale	___	**f**	believing in yourself
7	plump	___	**g**	having been artificially coloured
8	reserved	___	**h**	not kind
9	sociable	___	**i**	having skin darkened by the sun
10	tanned	___	**j**	light coloured

2 Read the paragraph and circle the correct words.

Many famous people got their lucky break in talent shows. It seems easy enough to do. The producers come to a town nearby and dozens of people sign (**1**) **up / in** for the competition. Of course, participants want to create a strong impression. Some contestants dress (**2**) **up / down** like real film stars, others come dressed in something more outrageous and wild. How you look doesn't really matter though; the most important thing is to show (**3**) **up / off** your talents and hope that the judges take (**4**) **over / to** you quickly. If you're truly talented, you shouldn't have any problem standing (**5**) **by / out** from the crowd. At the very least, you should try to have the most fun you can possibly have.

Unit 9

Develop your reading skills: understanding exemplification

1 Look at the main ideas in bold in each sentence. Underline the supporting examples.

1 Celebrities are often surrounded by **symbols of wealth**. For example, if you visit their luxurious homes, you will probably see expensive sports cars parked outside.

2 When **actors achieve fame**, the signs of attaining success aren't hard to spot. For instance, when they go out in public, the paparazzi may follow them or fans will approach them for autographs.

3 **A-list stars** are the most famous of actors, such as the ones who star in big Hollywood productions and the ones whose names always appear in the papers.

4 **Celebrities can find themselves in danger** due to their star status. One instance of this is when a stalker terrorises their everyday lives or when they receive threatening mail.

5 These simple **steps to success** are essential for any actor who wants to succeed in the world of acting. Firstly, an actor must work hard at his or her craft. Secondly, he or she must actively seek auditions. And thirdly, they need just a bit of luck.

6 They say that **nothing in life is free** and the **same applies to fame**. This can be seen in the way celebrities pay thousands of pounds to look their best, including the fees they must pay to managers, lawyers and personal assistants.

2 Circle the phrases from the sentences in exercise 1 which indicate that examples will follow.

3 Match the examples with the newspaper headlines.

> assaulted a fan ■ avoids the spotlight ■ best-selling book ■ creative writing professor
> ■ literary genius ■ lives in isolation ■ massive crowd ■ numerous unpaid bills
> ■ packed audience ■ record ticket sales ■ turns down award ■ uncontrolled aggressive behaviour

1
Famous Actor Arrested
_____
_____
_____

3
ARTIST REJECTS FAME
_____
_____
_____

2
Novelist to Receive Award
_____
_____
_____

4
SINGER'S CONCERT SELLS OUT
_____
_____
_____

4 Read these extracts from two different reviews of the same event and explain the main difference between them.

1
The awards ceremony took place in one of Los Angeles' most famous and luxurious cinema theatres on one of its most well-known streets. The occasion was marked by the presence of many great Hollywood actors and directors who attended the packed ceremony. The event was sponsored by a major Hollywood film studio with the help of other sponsors. The ceremony was held to honour Italy's contribution to American cinema.

2
The awards ceremony took place in the world famous Grauman's Chinese Theatre on Hollywood Boulevard. Attendees included Leonardo DiCaprio, Martin Scorsese, Robert de Niro, Francis Ford Coppola, Monica Bellucci and Nicholas Cage. The event was chiefly sponsored by Metro-Goldwyn-Mayer with the help of *Vanity Fair* and Gucci fashion house. The ceremony was held to honour 75 years of film-making contributions from American directors, actors, producers, screenwriters and composers of Italian heritage.

5 Which of the two extracts in exercise 4 is more successful in describing the event? Why?

6 Match the phrases with examples taken from exercise 4. Some phrases have more than one example.

1 cinema theatre	___	**a** Gucci fashion house
2 famous street	___	**b** Italian film people
3 actor/director	___	**c** Robert de Niro
4 main sponsor	___	**d** Metro-Goldwyn-Mayer
5 other sponsors	___	**e** *Vanity Fair*
6 those being honoured	___	**f** Francis Ford Coppola
		g Hollywood Boulevard
		h Grauman's Chinese Theatre
		i Monica Bellucci

7 Read the article and answer the questions.

Celebrities often create their own publicity. For example, many stars often alert the press of their plans for a night out ensuring that when they arrive there will be a crowd of photographers waiting to take their photograph, whether it's good or not. An even more extreme strategy to attract attention can be seen in celebrity weddings. The ceremony is usually covered by every major newspaper in the world and not just the big day itself but all the events leading up to it – the courtship, the wedding announcement, the enormous diamond ring, the pre-nuptial agreement and so on. By the time the two stars tie the knot, everyone is sick of hearing about it. Another instance of creating your own publicity is showing up at an awards ceremony wearing an outrageous or expensive outfit, one that will look good in photographs and be noticed. Journalists make a big fuss about whether or not the star was well dressed or not but, in the meantime, the star gets their photo in all the magazines. Of course, stars do occasionally go too far and they get stuck with a bad reputation, something that's harder to shake off than an unflattering photograph.

1 Name three things stars do to make their own publicity.

_____

2 Name three events that happen before a celebrity wedding.

_____

3 Name an example of what happens when a celebrity wears an expensive outfit.

_____

4 Name an example of something that's worse than a bad photograph.

_____

8 Read the article and choose the best sentence to fill each gap.

People find fame in many different ways – sometimes by taking risks, at other times fame springs from a related line of work and quite often it derives from family connections. **(1)** ___ In the 1950s, film star Jayne Mansfield – who at that time had very few film credits to her name – moved her entire family from Texas to Hollywood in order to pursue a film career. **(2)** ___ Other stars started out in modelling before hitting the big screen. **(3)** ___ The same goes for Kellan Lutz, star of the *Twilight* franchise, who modelled for Abercrombie & Fitch in his early days. **(4)** ___ Kate Hudson, daughter of award-winning actress Goldie Hawn, made a name for herself by giving a critically-acclaimed performance in *Almost Famous*. **(5)** ___ As you can see, there is never just one way to achieve your goals and the quest for fame is no exception.

a Charlize Theron, the star of such films as *Monster* and *Prometheus*, flew to Los Angeles on a one-way ticket when she was just 19 in the hope of becoming an actress.
b Some actors take huge risks in their search for stardom.
c Ashton Kutcher, star of television's *Two and a Half Men* as well as numerous films, began his career as a fashion model before finding fame as an actor.
d Both Will and Jada Pinkett Smith's children, Jaden and Willow, appeared in successful Hollywood films before they were even teenagers.
e Some of today's best-known actors already had one foot in the door because of their famous parents.

9 Which of the removed sentences in exercise 8 are examples which illustrate a point in the text? _____

10 Are these situations examples of the benefits (B) or drawbacks (D) of fame?

1 having the respect of people in your industry ___

2 earning lots of money by doing what you love ___

3 meeting other really famous people ___

4 not having to pay for designer clothes ___

5 being followed around by hundreds of people ___

6 seeing your face on the covers of magazines ___

7 having a large staff to take care of you ___

8 losing the ability to maintain your privacy ___

11 Tick the situations that are examples of an invasion of celebrity privacy.

1 photographing a celebrity at a film premiere ___

2 photographing a celebrity while they are shopping ___

3 asking a celebrity for an autograph ___

4 asking a celebrity how much money they make ___

5 filming a celebrity in their home from across the street ___

6 filming a celebrity with a mobile phone while they're dining out ___

7 getting a celebrity's phone number and calling them ___

8 getting a celebrity's address and sending them a fan letter ___

Exam focus:
understanding exemplification in *First*

1 Look at the exam practice section on page 76 and read the first paragraph. What does Katie's appearance serve as an example of?

a someone who works at a petrol station   **c** someone who lives in a small town

b someone who is not likely to be famous   **d** someone who is friendly and sociable

2 Read the extract from an article and answer the questions.

> Privacy is a serious issue for celebrities. Besides people snapping photos of them in their private moments, such as when they're having an early morning jog or driving their kids to school, some have complained that overly-devoted fans have even dug through their rubbish bins in search of a precious souvenir. Because of this, some celebrities take excessive precautions to safeguard their privacy. They use shredders to destroy any and all kinds of paperwork and some have even been known to burn items, or rather, have their assistants burn them, before putting
> *8* them into the rubbish bin. It might seem extreme but some famous people will do anything to stop any of their personal effects winding up in the hands of potentially dangerous 'admirers'.

1 An example of a serious issue celebrities have is

    A having their picture taken.

    B jogging in the morning.

    C having their private moments invaded.

    D having too much rubbish.

2 Celebrities taking their children to school is an example of

    A a serious issue.

    B a photo opportunity.

    C a particular complaint.

    D a private moment.

3 Which of the following is NOT an example of the 'excessive precautions' mentioned in the extract?

    A having an assistant

    B destroying documents

    C burning items

    D asking an assistant to destroy items

4 The word 'extreme' in line 8 refers to the behaviour of

    A dangerous admirers.

    B celebrity assistants.

    C celebrities.

    D devoted fans.

3 Write two examples from the text of each of the following ideas.

    1 private moments   _____

    2 extra precautions   _____

    3 celebrity admirers   _____

4 Match the parts of *First* Paper 1 with the strategies.

    1 Part 5 ___

    2 Part 6 ___

    3 Part 7 ___

    a An example in one sentence connects to a part of a previous sentence.

    b It's important to understand the details in order to find correct examples of it.

    c Understanding an example helps eliminate incorrect distractors.

Skills tip

In *First* Paper 1 Part 5, understanding exemplification is important for

a identifying the main idea of the text.   **Yes / No**

b understanding the writer's supporting ideas.

            Yes / No

Exam practice:
First Paper 1 Part 5

You are going to read a story about a woman who found fame. For questions 1–6, choose the answer (A, B, C or D) which you think fits best according to the text.

KATIE'S JOURNEY
to fame

Katie Kirkland wasn't what you would call celebrity material. She was of average height and slightly plump, with pale skin and dark, shoulder-length hair which she sometimes dyed light brown when she felt like doing something special for herself. She worked at a petrol station selling petrol, a job which she had done for the better part of her 35 years of life. She had a pleasant, round face with freckles. She was a sociable person with a warm smile and well known in her small town, mainly for her ability to sing. That was the one superstar trait Katie would ever possess.

On a chilly afternoon in March, a man pulled into Katie's petrol station to buy petrol. Katie, particularly cheerful that day, assisted the man by filling his car. She hummed a few lines of the Rolling Stones' *Satisfaction* while holding the petrol nozzle. The man, who recognised the famous tune, started singing the words. Katie joined in and the two of them sang the whole song together and had a great laugh. 'You've got an amazing voice. You really stand out from the crowd! Why are you working here?' said the man.

'Oh, thanks, but you know, I'm just a small-town girl. I'm not the celebrity type,' Katie replied with a shy smile.

The man left and returned the next day with a friend, a slim, tanned and well-dressed man, who asked Katie to come to his recording studio in the city. 'We'll arrange everything for you. We'll pick you up, record some songs and if at any point you don't feel comfortable about anything, we'll call it quits, no worries.' Katie was thrilled at the opportunity to show off her talents. She made arrangements to take a day off from work, travelled to the studio and recorded a few songs.

'You're absolutely brilliant! You've got to make an album. You're going to be a huge star, Katie!' exclaimed Mr White, the studio owner, who had taken to her straight away. Katie was beside herself with joy.

She took leave from her job and, over the next three weeks, she worked full-time recording songs. The studio owner set up a band and they recorded 12 songs. After a month of editing, the album hit the record shops and Katie's music caught on right away. Presenters on morning television programmes wanted to interview Katie and have her perform. As exciting as it all was, Katie felt reserved, as she didn't feel confident about her looks. The studio did its best to dress her up like a star, but she still didn't quite look the part. Critics praised her singing abilities but media criticism was harsh, even unfair, regarding her appearance. Nonetheless, Katie had an instant fan base, full of people who could relate to her normal looks and down-to-earth personality. However, the attention came at a steep price.

In a matter of months, Katie's life had gone from a simple, quiet existence to a thrilling wild ride and finally to what she considered to be a terrible curse. It wasn't what she had signed up for. The fans, who once were just adoring and appreciative, had turned into a mob. When Katie showed up for performances, people wanting autographs and photographs would swarm around her. They would come to her house at all hours of the day, hoping to catch a glimpse of her. Photographers began to publish unflattering pictures of Katie, which upset her beyond belief. Just when she thought she might go mad, she decided to take over the reins of her own life. With millions of pounds in album sales, Katie, taking the tanned man's words to heart, decided it was time to get away from celebrity life. She tearfully left her house, her friends, her whole life behind. The papers circulated headlines screaming 'Where's Katie?' but no-one could find her. Katie had decided her 15 minutes of fame were over. So soon after becoming a star, she travelled far, far away, where the burning lights of fame would never find her again.

70

1 What extraordinary feature does Katie have?

   A her hair style

   B her personality

   C her voice

   D her work ethic

2 Katie's response to the man's compliment was

   A reserved.

   B cheerful.

   C annoyed.

   D hopeful.

3 What do we learn about the tanned man's offer?

   A It was an offer Katie couldn't refuse.

   B There seemed to be a hidden agenda.

   C Katie was under no obligation to the man.

   D There were some things left out.

4 What was the reaction to Katie?

   A She received only positive reviews.

   B People thought her singing wasn't very good.

   C Her fans didn't like her appearance.

   D There was a mixed response.

5 Katie's stardom soon became

   A a dream come true.

   B a real nightmare.

   C a rags-to-riches story.

   D a boring and dull task.

6 The phrase '15 minutes of fame' in line 70 refers to

   A the exact amount of time Katie was in the spotlight.

   B the length of time that it took Katie to decide to leave.

   C the length of one of the songs from her album.

   D the short amount of time Katie spent as a celebrity.

Skills tip

Part 5 may include a question that asks you to refer to a specific line in the text. The question may ask about the meaning of a word or phrase that you probably won't know. The clues to the answer are included in the text that very closely surrounds the word or phrase. Read this part of the text very carefully and think about how the four choices fit (or don't fit) into the text.

10 Understanding text structure

Higher education

Improve your reading skills: understanding text structure

What is understanding text structure?

A well-written text has a clear structure. Argumentative texts often have an introduction, a main body where the argument is presented and a conclusion. Main points are presented in separate paragraphs, with examples, reasons, etc. Understanding text structure helps you to see how all the parts of a text work together. It involves distinguishing main ideas from supporting details (Unit 4), understanding purpose and function (Unit 5), understanding cohesion (Unit 6) and coherence (Unit 8), amongst other things.

1 Which of these statements is true?

   A All texts usually have introductions and conclusions.

   B A particular text type usually follows a typical structure.

Why is understanding text structure important?

Understanding text structure is important for each part of a text you read. It helps you to recognise and understand the function of each section. It is also important for your global understanding of a text. It's a key part of understanding the text.

2 Understanding text structure can help you to work out

   A what the writer thinks of a whole topic area.

   B what each part of the text does.

How do you understand text structure?

Make sure you are familiar with the kinds of structures we often see in different types of texts. For example, a newspaper or magazine article often begins with general background information, followed by key events or ideas, with examples and reasons, and it often ends with a personal comment from the writer.

3 Reports generally don't contain

   A long descriptive passages.

   B recommendations.

How is understanding text structure important in *First*?

In First Paper 1 Part 5, you may be asked questions about the text structure. These could include questions about what words refer to, or about how different parts of the text are connected. In Part 6, putting the removed sentences into the correct gaps involves understanding the function of the sentences and the structure of the whole text. In Part 7, statements about the texts may rely on understanding implication, attitude and opinion, comparison, exemplification, etc.

4 Understanding text structure helps you to

   A see how each part of the text is connected to the rest.

   B understand the whole text without reading the details.

Get started

Look at the photo and answer the questions.

- What are the advantages of higher education? Are there any disadvantages?
- Which of the following have you done or are you considering doing?
  - ☐ retraining for a job _____
  - ☐ studying for a degree _____
  - ☐ doing postgraduate studies _____
  - ☐ undertaking vocational training _____
  - ☐ having a gap year before university _____
  - ☐ starting your career straight after school _____
  - ☐ studying a subject because of its job prospects _____
  - ☐ doing some kind of apprenticeship or skills training _____

Develop your vocabulary

1 Circle the word or phrase that does not belong.

   1 to **get / have / gain / take / obtain** good marks
   2 to **get / make / find / be offered** a place on a course
   3 to **study / go / work hard / fall behind** at university
   4 to miss a **lesson / tutorial / lecture / course**

2 Complete the table.

Noun	Verb	Adjective
1 _____	qualify	**2** _____
		unqualified
graduate	**4** _____	
3 _____		
5 _____	educate	**6** _____
		uneducated

3 Read the paragraph and circle the correct words.

So I really don't know what to do for the best. My parents want me to go **(1) in / to / at** university and study **(2) in / at / for** a degree in law. They say that it's the best **(3) option / opinion / selection** if I want to enter the job **(4) career / profession / market** when I graduate. However, I don't know if I'm suited to another five years or more of study. And I'm worried that I'm not capable of studying at degree **(5) level / height / subjects**. I found my school exams really stressful and I don't know if I want to go through all that again.
What do you think?
Helen

Unit 10

Develop your reading skills: understanding text structure

1 Circle the correct word or phrase in each sentence.

1 Each room in the hall of residence is provided with a desk, a bed and a small toilet and shower area. **In addition / On the other hand**, there is cupboard space for clothes, a bookcase, a lamp and a notice board.

2 Recently, the British government passed a law allowing universities to charge up to a maximum of £9,000 a year for their fees. **For instance / Because of this**, many students are financially unable to undertake a degree course.

3 Your attendance at each lecture is not compulsory. **However / Also**, you are required to go to a minimum number of lectures for each course.

4 In Walker's youth, very few people went on to study at university level. **At that time / Furthermore**, higher education was reserved for the privileged few.

5 In some cases, taking a year off only delays your studies and won't look good on your CV. **It might be better to go / Once you have gone** to university straight from school if you don't have any specific plans for your gap year.

6 Students are usually offered a place at university which is conditional on achieving certain exam grades. **Before / After** that, the offer is either confirmed or withdrawn based on the student's actual exam results.

2 Write a word or phrase in bold from exercise 1 on each line to answer the questions. Which word/phrase helps to identify:

1 a reason?

_____

2 another similar point?

_____ _____ _____

3 an example?

_____

4 a contrasting idea?

_____ _____

5 a suggestion or recommendation?

_____

6 a sequence of events?

_____ _____ _____ _____

3 Choose the sentence, a or b, that follows most logically from the first sentence. In two of the items, both answers are correct.

1 Many jobs are available to students during the long summer vacation.
  a For instance, it would not be a good idea to work if it meant there was no time left for studying.
  b These include jobs in factories and seasonal work in the tourism industry.

2 Working while you are studying can help financially.
  a It can also teach you responsibility and give you useful work experience.
  b On the other hand, there is a danger that it will distract you from your studies.

3 All too often, employers look for some kind of work experience.
  a This can be frustrating for someone who has devoted their time to studying.
  b Despite the benefits of this, it will probably not help you find a job.

4 A year spent working between school and university can place you in a better position once you start a degree course.
  a You will probably have learned to be more organised and punctual, which can help you with your studies.
  b Students who do this tend to have a more mature approach to their course work.

5 The room I was given at college was incredibly small.
  a Furthermore, there was an amazing view from the window.
  b I remember once, when my brother visited, there was hardly enough room for him to sit at the table.

6 Giles wasted his years as a student.
  a Once he had got a place at a top university, he felt that he didn't need to do any more.
  b Despite this, he eventually failed his first-year exams and was quietly asked to leave.

4 Read the paragraphs and underline the topic sentence (the main idea) in each one.

a Although we tend to think of going to university when we talk about higher education, there is more to it than that. Vocational training, for example, is increasingly important. We have long recognised the need for an education which leads directly to a trade or profession and educational institutions are now offering more of such courses.

b A little less than 1,000 years ago, universities began to be popular throughout Europe. In the north, the focus was on the arts and religious subjects. Most of the teaching was done through the medium of Latin, and ancient texts, such as those by Aristotle and Hippocrates, were read. The number of educational establishments continued to grow, although by the end of the 18th century there were still fewer than 150 in the whole of Europe.

c The technological age has had a huge effect on education, with the rise of the internet making arguably the biggest difference. To take just one example, imagine how long it took scholars in the past to get access to information. They would have had to travel many miles – often to foreign lands – in search of the information they needed. This is in sharp contrast with today's scholars who have access to a vast amount of information freely available online.

d According to his autobiography, Charlton's college education was never about getting a job. He was determined to learn as much about life as his books and lecturers could teach him. He believed that it was his duty to surround himself with poetry, literature and great ideas. Whether or not that was useful to him afterwards was never a consideration.

5 Read the paragraphs in exercise 4 again and answer the questions. Which paragraph(s):

1 is argumentative? ____

2 are purely narrative? ____ ____

3 has a mixture of argumentative and narrative writing? ____

6 Underline the key words in the paragraphs that helped you find the answers to exercise 5.

7 Match each sentence with what it contains.
Then decide where they fit best in the paragraphs in exercise 4.

> **a** examples
> **b** feelings in a narrative
> **c** events in a narrative
> **d** contrasting ideas

1 He felt that the purpose of university was to make him a better person.

_____

2 Plumbers, electricians, chefs and nurses are all professionals who benefit from an education which is practical as well as theoretical.

_____

3 Southern universities, on the other hand, taught mainly law and medicine.

_____

4 They overcame a huge number of obstacles.

_____

8 The first sentence in each paragraph below is missing. Write a topic sentence for each one.

1 _____ First of all, his teachers had taken it for granted that he would. Then, as James later found out, his teachers had convinced his parents that he should apply to study at Oxford. 'I just didn't want to do it,' James explains, 'Everyone seemed to be deciding my future for me and nobody was thinking about what I wanted.' In the end, James did what everyone expected of him and was awarded a first class honours degree from Oxford. It was only later that he realised how useful this was.

2 _____ First of all, being in a study group means that you meet at regular times and you are more likely to get something done. Secondly, you are able to share the opinions of others, which can help you to think more deeply about a subject. Then, you can often learn things more quickly than you would on your own. In addition, you can pick up new study skills from other group members. However, it's important to ask yourself if the members of the group are serious about what they're doing. A poor study group is unlikely to help you that much.

9 Write a sentence to say what the paragraphs in exercise 8 are about.

1 _____

2 _____

10 Decide whether each paragraph in exercise 8 is narrative or discursive.
Underline words or phrases that helped you decide.

1 ___   **2** ___

11 Complete the sentences with ideas of your own.
  1 Studying alone helps you to concentrate on your work. However, …
  2 Going to university is definitely a good idea. First of all, …
  3 Paul couldn't decide whether to study literature or something more practical. In the end, …
  4 Online courses are a good solution for some students. This includes people who …
  5 There is no reason why you can't have a great social life at college. If you can …
  6 Sarah was extremely nervous about leaving her family and taking up a place at university. Once she got there, …

Exam focus:
understanding text structure in *First*

1 Look at the exam practice section on page 84 and answer the questions.

   1 What is the text about? What type of writing is it? _____

   2 Identify sections of the text where the writer talks about:

- the benefits of having a higher education: Paragraphs __ __ __ __
- the negative aspects of higher education: Paragraphs __ __ __
- narrative writing (in the past tense): Paragraphs __ __
- your choice of degree course: Paragraphs __ __ __
- money: Paragraph __

> **Skills tip**
>
> In *First* Paper 1 Part 6, does understanding text structure help you
>
> **a** follow the writer's argument?   **Yes / No**
>
> **b** find detailed information?
>   **Yes / No**

2 Read the short extracts below and look at the gaps and the phrases in bold. Answer the questions.

   1 When you are a first-year student at university, there is so much going on socially that you might get into **difficulty**. `1` `___` **To avoid this**, it's a good idea to make a study plan and stick to it.
What kind of difficulty might the writer be talking about? What might you want to avoid?

   2 It is worth looking at universities which have the **best graduate employment records**. `2` `___` **However**, you might be surprised to know that neither Oxford nor Cambridge made the top ten last year.
Is the missing sentence likely to be about good universities or bad ones?

   3 There is always a danger that your qualifications will **not help you find a job**. `3` `___` Graduates in archaeology were **similarly unsuccessful**.
Is the missing sentence likely to be about degrees which lead to a job, or degrees which do not lead to a job? What could archaeology graduates be similar to? What does 'unsuccessful' probably refer to?

   4 **Distance learning courses have several distinct advantages**. First of all, you do not need to move away from home. Secondly, you do not have to travel to lectures or tutorials – everything you need is on your computer. `4` `___`
What kind of information would you expect to find in the gap?

3 Match each sentence with the correct gap in exercise 2.

   a Some of them frequently report that 90% or more of their graduates have found a job within six months.

   b These factors could save you considerable amounts of time and money.

   c Joining clubs and societies, as well as socialising with a new group of friends, could mean that you fall behind with your course work.

   d A recent study in the USA found that the worst choice of degree major was anthropology, with high unemployment rates and low salaries among graduates.

4 Tick the statements that are true about *First* Paper 1. Understanding text structure helps you

   1 understand what certain words refer to in Part 5.   ___

   2 see how different parts of the text are connected in Part 6. ___

   3 understand the writer's attitude and opinion in Part 7.   ___

   4 find examples and reasons in Part 7.   ___

Exam practice:
First Paper 1 Part 6

You are going to read an article about higher education. Six sentences have been removed from the article. Choose from the sentences A–G the one which fits each gap (1–6). There is one extra sentence which you do not need to use.

IS HIGHER EDUCATION
for everyone?

Everyone tells you the same thing – work hard at school so that you can go on to study at a university or college. It seems to be sensible advice. After all, the more qualified you are, the better chance you have of getting a good job, right? Higher education is always a good thing, isn't it?

Firstly, it depends on what you're planning to study. In terms of being employable when you graduate, the different branches of medicine, including dentistry, are probably the safest choices. Some studies show that close to 100% of graduates in these fields found a job within six months. **1** [ ]

On the other hand, if it is your dream to study history or sociology, you need to be aware that, at the moment, you are less likely to find a job if your degree is in either of these subjects. **2** [ ] Once they graduated, many were unable to find work. Others were forced to undertake more years of study or retraining in order to enter the job market.

Degrees related to business and management are among the most popular at the moment, which means there is a great deal of competition for places both at university and at work. So you may not find a place on your chosen course and, if you do, you will graduate with the same qualifications as thousands of other people. To avoid this you might consider studying more specialised subjects such as waste management or environmental management. They may not be your first choice but they are among the newer kinds of courses on offer which could well lead to a good job. **3** [ ]

Because, let's face it, not everyone is suited to another three or four years of study. Some people are better off not continuing their education. **4** [ ] In addition, your family's financial circumstances might make it difficult to go away to study. Furthermore, some people simply can't afford the expense of it all.

This brings us to the all-important subject of money. The average graduate with a bachelor's degree owes in excess of £15,000 and this figure is increasing every year. If one also considers the fact that he or she typically has to wait at least three months before he or she starts earning, you can see that spending those extra three or four years actually earning money can make quite a difference. **5** [ ]

Of course, despite all this, there are still many benefits of studying at degree level. **6** [ ] And graduates usually get paid higher salaries. In the end, the advice to work hard at school is sound advice. No-one in their right mind would tell you to do the opposite. Leaving school with good qualifications will at least give you more options. What you do with those options is up to you.

A However, you have to ask yourself if it's worth spending several years of your life studying something that is less than ideal for you.

B If you can find a job at 18 (or, why not, at 16), then you could end up being much more financially secure.

C Law graduates were similarly successful, so if these subjects are really what you want to study and you can get a place on a course you are lucky.

D These include people who suffer terribly from exam nerves, and those who find academic work really difficult.

E This would mean moving to the other end of the country or even to a different country altogether.

F A degree that is not in demand is practically useless, as many recent graduates have found out to their cost.

G A large number of employers look for some evidence of higher education.

Skills tip

When you do *First* Paper 1 Part 6, understanding text structure will help you to follow the writer's arguments; identify different sections of the text; find examples and reasons to support the main topic of a paragraph; notice when the writer changes direction or begins a new subject. All of these will help you choose the correct sentences to fill the gaps.

11

Understanding comparison

Technology in the home

UNIT AIMS

Skill: understanding comparison

Vocabulary: technology topic vocabulary

Exam practice: *First* Paper 1 Part 7

Improve your reading skills: understanding comparison

What is understanding comparison?

Writers often make comparisons. They try to explain things by comparing something the reader doesn't know about with something the reader does know about. Understanding comparison means recognising different kinds of comparison and understanding what is being compared.

1 Comparisons may be used to

   A show how little some readers know.

   B explain something in terms you understand.

Why is understanding comparison important?

It is an important part of understanding what a writer is trying to explain. If you don't recognise and understand a comparison, you won't fully understand that part of the text. You may confuse the topic with an idea which is being used for comparison.

2 By understanding comparison, you are more likely to understand

   A topics.

   B confusion.

How do you understand comparison?

A key part of understanding comparison is to recognise commonly used expressions. These include phrases such as in comparison, is like *and* is similar to. *They also include grammatical structures such as comparative and superlative forms and* as ... as. *They also include metaphors and similes.*

3 Which of these sentences does NOT contain a comparison?

   A Tablet computers will soon be as popular as laptops.

   B Most teenagers don't like strict rules about their use of technology.

How is understanding comparison important in *First*?

Understanding comparison is relevant to Parts 5, 6 and 7 of First *Paper 1. In Part 5, comparisons may tell you about the writer's attitude or opinion and help you understand specific details. In Part 6, a removed sentence may draw a comparison with something in the main text. In Part 7, you may be asked to match a statement to a text based on a comparison.*

4 In Part 5, comparisons in a text may reveal

   A which questions are easier than others.

   B what a writer feels about a subject.

Get started

Look at the photo and answer the questions.

- What does the picture show?
- What are the benefits of this kind of household technology?
- Are homes with smart technology better for the environment? Why? / Why not?
- Would you like to live in this kind of home? Why? / Why not?

Develop your vocabulary

1 Circle the correct word in each sentence.

1 The remote control uses **digital / latest** technology.
2 You should use a low temperature washing **set / programme** for delicate fabrics.
3 A vacuum cleaner is a labour-saving **machine / device**.
4 Video players are **obsolete / extinct** nowadays.
5 A good security **structure / system** helps to prevent burglaries.
6 This smartphone has a **revolutionary / basic** new design.
7 You can **contact / operate** the DVD player manually or by remote control.

2 Write a word from the box in each gap to complete the text.

> computerised ■ conventional ■ efficient ■ features
> ■ gadgets ■ models ■ programmed ■ state-of-the-art

When choosing one of our (**1**) _____ kitchens you will find everything you need and more. Our designs contain many (**2**) _____ that are not normally found in other more (**3**) _____ kitchens. Firstly, the fridge-freezer has a (**4**) _____ control panel that automatically adjusts the settings depending on how full it is. Our fabulous built-in cookers are self-cleaning and the oven can be (**5**) _____ so that you can time exactly when your cooking starts and finishes. The dishwasher is highly (**6**) _____ and saves both energy and water when cleaning your dishes. And finally, all the kitchen (**7**) _____ are the latest (**8**) _____ available on the market.

Unit 11

Develop your reading skills: understanding comparison

1 Write a word from the box in each gap.

> as ■ compared ■ comparison ■ like ■ same ■ similar

1 An e-reader is _____ to a tablet computer.

2 Her new carpet cleaner looks a bit _____ a modern steam engine!

3 In _____ to conventional light bulbs, these ones are much more energy efficient.

4 Wide screen TVs are very cheap _____ to their price even a year ago.

5 He thinks the sound quality of digital music isn't as good _____ that on old vinyl records.

6 Cordless kettles work in the _____ way as an ordinary one does.

2 Write the complete phrase used to make each of the comparisons in exercise 1.

1 _____   4 _____

2 _____   5 _____

3 _____   6 _____

3 Read the definitions and circle the correct answer.

1 *a phrase that describes something by comparing it to something else using the word 'like' or 'as'*
This is a metaphor / simile.

2 *a word or phrase that means one thing and is used to refer to another thing in order to emphasise their similar qualities*
This is a metaphor / simile.

4 Decide if the phrases in bold are similes (S) or metaphors (M).

1 Your new coffee maker **looks like something out of *Star Wars*!** ___

2 It's **as cold as ice** in here. Why don't you turn on the heating? ___

3 The designer has incorporated geothermal heating into the new house – **it's very like the system the ancient Romans** used to heat their public baths. ___

4 My new smart fridge can tell me exactly what shopping I need and even create recipes – **it's magic**. ___

5 I'll have to get someone to come and set up the new computer system, I'm too busy and **time is money**. ___

6 The touch screen on my new mobile is **as hard as nails** – nothing can break or scratch it. ___

5 Read the short texts and decide if the statements are true (T) or false (F).

> Even when there is a recession, factories are creating all kinds of new home technology products. Manufacturers clearly don't sit around with time on their hands – when consumers are ready to start spending again, hundreds of new products will be ready for sale.

1 Manufacturers must use their hands in a certain way to create their products. ____

2 Companies are busy developing new home technology products. ____

> A robot that cleans your house is every homeowner's dream but the laser vacuum cleaner takes the idea a step further. The new model features a laser which makes a map of your house, allowing the vacuum cleaner to navigate around furniture and see which areas of the house are still dirty.

3 The idea for this household appliance came to its inventor in a dream. ____

4 Everyone who has a house would like to own the new laser vacuum cleaner. ____

> Which busy mother doesn't wish she had another pair of hands to rock the baby at the same time as doing jobs around the house? The new electronic baby rocker moves like you do and can also mimic the movement of a swing or a car ride. This new gadget will become a second mother to your child!

5 The baby rocker moves in the same way as a mother rocking her baby. ____

6 With this device your child can have two mothers. ____

6 Read the paragraph and circle the correct words.

> This food processor is a bit (**1**) **similar / like** a space-age gadget for preparing food. Not (**2**) **only / also** does it perform more functions than ordinary blenders, but it (**3**) **also / only** does them better. It is similar (**4**) **as / to** the type of processor used by chefs in professional kitchens but it requires no special skills to use it. You will have (**5**) **much / more** room in your kitchen because with this clever tool you won't need (**6**) **like / as** many different appliances as before. It can chop, grate, blend, mix and slice – in fact it's your best friend! Your sauces, soups, cakes and desserts will be (**7**) **best / better** than ever and will take half the time to make. It could just be the (**8**) **more / most** important kitchen appliance you will ever buy.

7 Read the paragraph in exercise 6 again and find examples of these kinds of comparison.

1 comparatives _____

2 a superlative _____

3 a metaphor _____

4 a simile _____

5 *as ... as* structure _____

8 Read the text and decide if the statements are true (T) or false (F).

What will the homes of the future be like? They will have little in common with the homes we live in today. In order to become more environmentally friendly, they may be built underground, like animal dens, in order to conserve energy. Another development which will be seen more and more frequently is the technique of building the walls and roofs from photovoltaic panels. These panels, which look like large black slabs, can create more electricity than the homes need, allowing homeowners to sell surplus electricity back to electricity companies. The interiors of modern homes will have the most advanced robotics and smart technology people can afford. A central control panel will operate heating and lighting and the wealthiest people will programme robots to do all the cooking and cleaning. With more leisure time people will have a much better quality of life. Homes will be designed as our own personal worlds. They will be places to live, work and be entertained in and, unlike today, we will have little need to leave them unless we want to.

1 Homes of the future will be very similar to the ones we live in now.   ____

2 Homes could mimic the way animals build their homes.   ____

3 Underground homes will reduce the amount of electricity people use.   ____

4 Photovoltaic panels will provide some of the electricity for homes of the future.   ____

5 How advanced the technology in people's homes is will depend on how rich they are.   ____

6 An increase in free time will mean an improvement in people's lives.   ____

7 The homes of the future will make people more independent.   ____

9 Write one word in each gap to complete the text.

The world of home entertainment has moved on spectacularly (1) _____ comparison to the electronic appliances of the past. Now there is no need for separate systems, such as a DVD player, a TV and a stereo. All you need is a computer, a good screen and speakers. Compared (2) _____ installing lots of separate systems, a home entertainment system is easy to set up and your living room will look (3) _____ tidier without having so many cables everywhere. And (4) _____ best thing of all is that, with such good sound and picture quality, your living room will be (5) _____ a cinema and concert hall rolled into one!

10 Read the text in exercise 9 again and answer the questions.

1 What is the main difference between entertainment systems of the past and the present?

_____

2 Why will living rooms be tidier with a modern home entertainment system?

_____

3 What is a modern home entertainment system compared to?

_____

_____

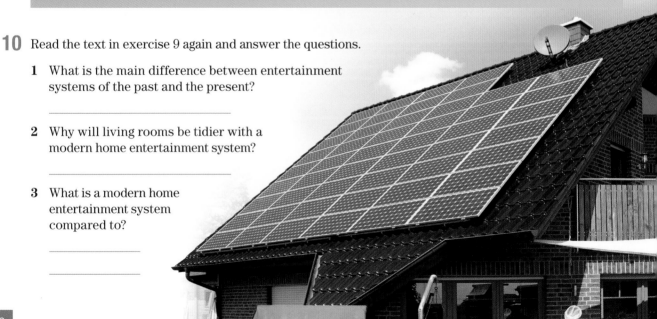

Exam focus:
understanding comparison in *First*

1 Look at the exam practice section on page 92. Which of the questions make use of comparative structures? Underline the key words and phrases used.

2 Tick the sentences that use comparison.

1 The new airport is like a great big, high-tech shopping centre. ____

2 Surprisingly, there were no winners in the recent competition. ____

3 My partner doesn't like speaking about his work. ____

4 Sarah had a similar experience to that with her video camera last year. ____

5 Just as the popularity of loud music has risen sharply, so too has the incidence of hearing loss among teenagers. ____

6 You should always compare prices online before buying. ____

7 I think the contrast on the screen is wrong. ____

8 Paul is not as good with computers as his sister Leanne. ____

3 Look at the sentences which you ticked in exercise 2 and decide what kind of comparison they use.

a a comparative structure _____

b a simile (using *like*) _____

c using a word for comparison _____

> ## Skills tip
>
> In *First* Paper 1 Part 7, the ability to accurately identify comparisons
>
> a can help you match the questions with the correct text. **Yes / No**
>
> b could be confusing when trying to match questions to texts. **Yes / No**
>
> c can make understanding the meaning in a text easier. **Yes / No**

4 Match the texts with the questions.

A Smartphones

With the early widespread use of mobile phones came a common complaint. Mobile phones were inhibiting the development of real communication and meaningful friendships, as people were constantly interrupting face-to-face conversations in order to answer texts and to make calls. So how much worse is it today with the advent of smartphones and other touch screen devices? Everyone has some kind of multi-purpose gadget that can be used for communication, playing music and games or surfing the net. But have our relationships really suffered as a result? I believe they're as good as they ever were.

B Television

Thanks to advertising for television shows and DVDs created for babies, many parents believe that watching educational programmes will stimulate their babies' brains and actually improve learning. Many parents seem to accept this idea. They believe that exposing a baby to educational DVDs will put him or her on to an early path to a highly-developed intelligence. Maybe not. A new study has shown that babies who spent more time in front of the TV actually performed worse in language and skills tests than those babies who watched less.

In which text does the writer

1 explain that a technological gadget is not beneficial? ____

2 compare the present with the recent past? ____

3 express the view that things have not changed for the worse? ____

4 compare two different groups and kinds of behaviour? ____

5 compare the way people socialise now with the past? ____

91

Exam practice:
First Paper 1 Part 7

You are going to read an article about technology in the home.
For questions 1–10, choose from the texts (A–D). The texts may be chosen more than once.

Which text

mentions the variety of different appliances available?	**1**
explains how one device can be used instead of many others?	**2**
emphasises how much people in the past would have liked this modern appliance?	**3**
compares a domestic appliance to something used for road maintenance?	**4**
says that a domestic task in the past required a great deal of physical strength?	**5**
mentions how the most up-to-date homes are now organised?	**6**
contrasts the ecological benefits of a modern appliance to methods of the past?	**7**
refers to an appliance from the past that took a long time to prepare before it could be used?	**8**
makes a prediction about a particular device?	**9**
describes a modern appliance as being similar to a servant?	**10**

Skills tip

In *First* Paper 1 Part 7, the questions may refer to a comparison made in the reading texts. The ability to quickly scan and identify comparisons will help you to match a question to a particular reading text. Read the questions and underline any key words or phrases connected with comparisons. Scan the reading texts looking for any words, phrases or structures used to make comparisons and then check these against the comparisons you have identified in the question.

THE ROAD TO
domestic bliss

How has household technology revolutionised life in the home?

A The washing machine

In days gone by, there were few chores more back-breaking than doing the laundry. For centuries, heavy, wet clothing and sheets had to be cleaned by hand with no other help than a washboard and a mangle. These were the nearest thing to a washing machine and a dryer. The washboard was simply a board with ridges on it that made scrubbing clothes easier and a mangle used two rollers to squeeze excess water out of cloth, a bit like a steam roller that is used to flatten the tarmac on highways!

But there is simply no comparison between a washboard and mangle and a modern washing machine. Not only is the washing machine highly efficient and easy to use, it also saves on water, so it is more environmentally friendly than washing by hand. There is little doubt that the housewives of the past would have been delighted to use a modern washing machine with its wide range of washing programmes.

B The cooker

You could say that choosing a cooker is as complicated as deciding what kind of car to get these days. There are so many different types of cookers and ovens – gas or electric, with or without a fan oven, a microwave oven with or without a conventional grill. The list of features is endless and, just as is the case for so many household appliances these days, many use digital technology and are computerised, too.

It's a far cry from the days when a pot was hung over a fire or when the cook had to use wood or coal to light a stove or cooking range and heat it for hours before it could even be used. Now cookers heat up instantly and many of the latest models can even be programmed to turn themselves on and off when you're not there.

C The vacuum cleaner

Wall-to-wall carpets are now a feature of many homes but they would be very difficult to keep clean, if it weren't for vacuum cleaners. The first electrical carpet cleaners using suction appeared at the beginning of the last century and have undergone many refinements since then. Advances in robotics have resulted in vacuum cleaners that can clean all the rooms in a house without the need for a human to operate them. They are like a high-tech housemaid and have proved a real labour-saving device for families everywhere.

Before vacuum cleaners became available and affordable for all, cleaning rugs and carpets meant either sweeping them with a stiff brush or hanging them over a line outside and beating the dirt out of them with a large stick or wooden paddle. You needed the muscles of a weightlifter to get your carpets clean back then. Today, you hardly have to lift a finger.

D The computer

Now found in nearly every home, the computer is the device that has had the most revolutionary effect on how we lead our lives. And just as it has affected today's domestic technology, so too will it affect the domestic appliances of the future. Computers have begun to replace many other devices around the home, making them obsolete. Computers are increasingly used for entertainment and communication, for shopping and work and as a way of controlling other systems and devices in the home. Who needs all those gadgets of the past, such as a sound system or DVD recorder, when the computer can perform all their functions and more? State-of-the-art homes now use computer technology to run almost every aspect of domestic life, from controlling the heating to automatically ordering food from the supermarket. And computers are likely to play an ever-increasing role in how we run our homes in the future.

12

Understanding implication

Imprisonment

UNIT AIMS

Skill: understanding implication

Vocabulary: social issues topic vocabulary

Exam practice: *First* Paper 1 Part 5

Improve your reading skills: understanding implication

What is understanding implication?	*Some things are not stated clearly in a text. However, they may be implied. For example, if a writer says, 'Prison taught me a lot.', we can reasonably assume that the writer was convicted of a crime, even though it's not explicit. Understanding implication means seeing what is behind the things a writer says.*

1 When something is implied,

    A it isn't stated explicitly in a text.

    B it is because the writer is trying to hide it.

Why is understanding implication important?	*Writers expect that we will understand some things without being told explicitly. If we don't recognise and understand things that are implied, we will only understand part of the text and we might miss something important.*

2 If you don't understand implication, you might

    A not understand something stated explicitly.

    B miss an important piece of information.

How do you understand implication?	*Read a text carefully and ask yourself questions about it. 'If what the writer says is true, what else must, logically, be true? What does the writer want me to understand, even though he or she hasn't said it explicitly? What is being implied here?' Then, consider these things as you read the rest of the text and check your understanding against both explicit and implicit information.*

3 As you read, you need to keep checking that

    A you understand what has been implied.

    B any new information is in fact true.

How is understanding implication important in *First*?	*It is important in* First *Paper 1 Parts 5, 6 and 7. In Part 5, you may be asked specific questions about things that are implied in the text. In Part 6, removed sentences may be connected to something that is implied in the text. In Part 7, you may need to understand attitude or opinion and this may be implied, rather than stated explicitly.*

4 Understanding implication is useful for understanding

    A what is implied in the questions in Part 5.

    B attitude and opinion in Part 7.

Get started

Look at the photo and answer the questions.

- Why might this man be in this situation?
- How do you think he might be feeling?
- What do you think his typical day is like?

Develop your vocabulary

1 Match to make phrases.

1	crime	___	**a**	confinement
2	hardened	___	**b**	criminal
3	justice	___	**c**	offence
4	life	___	**d**	rate
5	minor	___	**e**	sentence
6	solitary	___	**f**	system

2 Write a word from the box in each gap to complete the sentences.

> charge ■ commit ■ convict ■ finds ■ sentence

1 If the jury _____ you guilty, the judge will send you to prison.

2 Nobody should be able to _____ a crime without facing the consequences.

3 The police didn't _____ him with anything as they had no proof.

4 The jury can't _____ her of murder – she wasn't in the country at the time.

5 'Since it's your first offence,' said the judge, 'I'll only _____ you to six months in prison.'

3 Read the paragraph and circle the correct words.

○ Guilty verdict **for businessman** ○

The **(1) jury / judge** in the case of businessman Ken Ruddle have reached a guilty verdict. They were not convinced by the **(2) lawyer's / cellmate's** argument that his client was not guilty of **(3) bribery / shoplifting** and that the money he gave to a government official was in the form of a loan. Judge Margaret Reynolds ruled that the Canadian businessman should stay behind **(4) bars / walls** until she was ready to pass **(5) sentence / punishment** next week. She warned Ruddle that, in light of the seriousness of the offence, he should expect a term of **(6) prison / imprisonment**.

Develop your reading skills: understanding implication

1 Read the sentences and tick what is implied.

1 The judge sentenced him to life imprisonment.

   a He had been found guilty of a serious crime. ____

   b He was unfairly treated by the judge. ____

2 Most prisoners are keen to learn new skills in prison.

   a Many prisoners find good jobs on release from prison. ____

   b Some prisoners have no interest in improving themselves. ____

3 While in prison, Keith learned to stand up for himself.

   a People in prison tried to threaten Keith. ____

   b People in prison tried to teach Keith things. ____

4 A ten-year sentence is excessive for a crime such as shoplifting.

   a The punishment should fit the crime. ____

   b You shouldn't go to jail for shoplifting. ____

5 Olivia found the first few months inside the worst.

   a Olivia enjoyed prison after the first few months. ____

   b Olivia got more used to prison as time passed. ____

2 Match the sentences with what they imply.

1 This was his tenth offence, but the first time he had spent any time behind bars. ____

2 The people who say prisons are like hotels have never spent time in one. ____

3 A prison officer can't be a father, counsellor and teacher, too. ____

4 What chance does someone have re-entering the world after a ten-year sentence? ____

5 Prisons are often said to be a criminal's university. ____

a The writer has been in prison.
b Ex-convicts very often end up back in prison.
c The justice system is soft on offenders.
d Minor offenders often find out in prison how to carry out serious crimes.
e Prisons need specialist staff to help prisoners.

3 Read the paragraph and tick the statements which are implied.

> The door closed behind him and Reeves was left alone. He looked at the cell, finding it much as he had expected from watching TV. There was a bunk bed, a desk, a toilet. No cellmate, as least not for the moment. The prison officer had told him someone would arrive later. At least there would be a chance for him to collect his thoughts a little. Everything had happened so quickly since the judge passed that fateful sentence of life in prison. His lawyer had had the decency to look ashamed. He knew Reeves was innocent by then, but now Reeves understood why his brother had urged him to find the money to pay for a lawyer, by whatever means necessary.

1 Reeves had never been to prison before. ____

2 Reeves would be sharing a cell. ____

3 Reeves felt very shaken by his experience. ____

4 Reeves' lawyer was upset with the judge. ____

5 Reeves' lawyer had done a bad job. ____

6 Reeves had not paid his lawyer. ____

4 Match each sentence with the tone of the writer. There is an extra word that you do not need to use.

> angry ■ humorous ■ regretful ■ sad ■ sarcastic

1 I suppose what pass as necessities in prison today are en-suite showers, internet access, colour TVs in every cell and a weekly visit from the prison barber. _____

2 What a disgrace that we feel it is acceptable to put people in solitary confinement for weeks on end. How exactly are such inhuman conditions meant to make anyone a useful member of society? _____

3 The prisoners had made Christmas presents for their kids and one of them dressed as Santa Claus and distributed the presents. After he had finished playing his role, he waved goodbye to the guards and headed towards the visitors' exit. _____

4 I wish I had tried to reach my son sooner. By the time I got in touch he was so angry and resentful that he hardly wanted to listen. _____

5 Read the sentences from exercise 4 again and tick what is implied.

1 **a** Prisoners are treated too easily these days. ____

   b Prisoners are treated too harshly these days. ____

2 **a** People should not be kept in solitary confinement for as long as they are. ____

   b We must make sure solitary confinement is never used in prisons. ____

3 **a** A prisoner played a joke. ____

   b A prisoner tried to escape. ____

4 **a** The writer and his son have a good relationship. ____

   b The writer and his son have a bad relationship. ____

6 Read the paragraphs and decide whether each idea is expressed explicitly (E) or implicitly (I).

1 The main problem with prison is boredom. I should know, I've spent enough time behind bars. The worst of it is when you're young, because you're so full of energy. Half of the trouble I got into was just the result of working off the energy that had built up in me from sitting in a cell twenty-three hours a day. The other half was pure stupidity and stubbornness.

   a The writer has spent many years in prison. ____

   b The writer was a youth when he first went to prison. ____

2 Almost every writer who talks about their experience in prison makes some reference to the sky. It is usually blue, infinite. Sometimes a bird flies up there and this pulls hardest at the prisoner's heartstrings. No free man attaches quite so much significance to such an everyday sight.

   a The sky stands as a symbol of freedom to all prisoners. ____

   b There are a number of people who have written about their time in jail. ____

3 I've visited many prisons in my time and spoken to many prisoners. What struck me for the most part was how little of what they did was their fault. They had a bad upbringing, the teachers at school failed them, the police were always out to get them. Some even blamed God. Often they were completely innocent and wanted me to help them to get out. But even those who admitted they were guilty as charged still felt they deserved to be free.

   a The information the writer has about prisoners was often gained from first hand. ____

   b The writer has very little sympathy for the people he has met in prison. ____

7 Read the paragraphs in exercise 6 again and choose the correct answers.

1 Who does the writer of paragraph 1 blame for the trouble he got into as a youth in prison?
  a himself
  b the prison system
  c both himself and the system

2 How does the writer feel about free men in paragraph 2?
  a They don't make connections with what they see around them.
  b They fail to appreciate the freedom that they enjoy.
  c They have no intention of going back to prison.

3 What does the writer imply about convicts in paragraph 3?
  a Very few of them are willing to take responsibility for their own actions.
  b Many of them are in prison for crimes they did not commit.
  c We should take a hard look at the system before we condemn them.

8 Read the letter and circle the sentences that fit best.

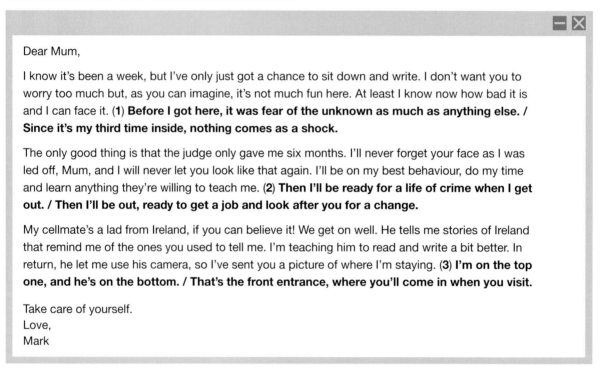

Dear Mum,

I know it's been a week, but I've only just got a chance to sit down and write. I don't want you to worry too much but, as you can imagine, it's not much fun here. At least I know now how bad it is and I can face it. **(1) Before I got here, it was fear of the unknown as much as anything else. / Since it's my third time inside, nothing comes as a shock.**

The only good thing is that the judge only gave me six months. I'll never forget your face as I was led off, Mum, and I will never let you look like that again. I'll be on my best behaviour, do my time and learn anything they're willing to teach me. **(2) Then I'll be ready for a life of crime when I get out. / Then I'll be out, ready to get a job and look after you for a change.**

My cellmate's a lad from Ireland, if you can believe it! We get on well. He tells me stories of Ireland that remind me of the ones you used to tell me. I'm teaching him to read and write a bit better. In return, he let me use his camera, so I've sent you a picture of where I'm staying. **(3) I'm on the top one, and he's on the bottom. / That's the front entrance, where you'll come in when you visit.**

Take care of yourself.
Love,
Mark

9 Read the letter in exercise 8 again. Write five inferences we can make from it.

1 _____

2 _____

3 _____

4 _____

5 _____

Exam focus:
understanding implication in *First*

1 Think about *First* Paper 1 Part 5 and tick the statements that are true.
Understanding implication will help you

  1 with questions about the consequences of actions in the text. ____

  2 to see what word is a synonym of one in the text. ____

  3 to understand the attitude of the writer to ideas in the text. ____

  4 to comprehend the general meaning of a paragraph. ____

  5 to know what word a particular pronoun refers to. ____

Skills tip

In *First* Paper 1 Part 5,
should you use your first
quick read through

a to underline words
  whose meaning you
  are unsure of?   **Yes / No**
b to get a good impression
  of what the writer feels
  about the issues raised?
                   Yes / No

2 Read the paragraph and answer the question.

> We seem to have forgotten the whole idea of youthful indiscretion. How
> many of us have done something in our youth that could have resulted
> in a criminal charge, such as stealing a chocolate bar or buying alcohol
> underage, to name a couple of examples familiar to me? This is not to say
> that these should not be illegal – of course they should. But should they
> really be cause for being jailed, for an end to the offender's education, for
> a stigma that will follow him or her around for the next 50 years, blocking
> job opportunities, careers in the public service, even voting rights?

What can you infer from the paragraph?
a The writer thinks the readers don't remember their youth.
b The writer believes that young offenders get off too lightly.
c The writer has spent time in an institution for young offenders.
d The writer has committed minor offences as a youth.

3 Match the incorrect answers from the question in exercise 2 with the
reasons they were incorrect.

  1 This is the opposite of the point the writer is making. ____

  2 The writer did things that 'could have resulted' in a
     conviction, not things that *did* result in a conviction. ____

  3 The writer says this explicitly, not implicitly. ____

4 Choose the correct ending to complete each sentence.
  1 In *First* Paper 1 Part 6, understanding implication will help you
     a recognise implicit content in missing sentences.
     b understand what reference words in missing sentences link to.
  2 In *First* Paper 1 Part 7, understanding implication will help you
     a match less obvious elements such as attitude and opinion.
     b spot rephrased elements from the texts in the questions.

Exam practice:
First Paper 1 Part 5

You are going to read an article about private prisons. For questions 1–6,
choose the answer (A, B, C or D) which you think best fits according to the text.

ARE PRIVATE PRISONS
the solution?

With a proven preference for all things privatised, the government is turning its eye
on prisons again. But can America's experience teach us something?

There are now around 100,000 prisoners in private prisons in the US, ranging from young offender institutions to high security facilities for the most hardened criminals: murderers and those who have committed other serious crimes. The prison population in the US has seen a small decrease over the past two years, after decades of consistent and continuous growth. This is partly due to a drop in crime rates and partly from a general recognition on the part of state and federal government that putting petty criminals behind bars was the least effective way to deal with crime. It is, however, bad news for private prisons.

Private prisons are run like any other business, which means they need customers. What is unusual about them, though, is that their customers don't really want to use their services; the criminal who volunteers to go to jail is the exception to the rule. The private prison system relies on the justice system of judges, juries and lawyers to provide them with the customers they need in order to remain profitable. This means that there is a group pushing for longer and more frequent prison sentences that is not motivated by ideology, but by money.

It leads to some deep conflicts of interest for governments, the justice system and the general public. Two of the biggest private prison companies have been involved in lobbying the government for longer sentences and for the creation of new crimes. One extreme case involved bribery: two judges were paid to send 2,000 youths to a private prison for juvenile offenders, some for offences as minor as stealing some DVDs. There are also whole towns that depend on their prisons for employment, which creates an unhealthy need for prisoners in the wider community. Such towns have often helped build the private prisons with public or, more often, borrowed money, in an effort to attract the private prison company. If the company decides the prison no longer makes financial sense, they may pull out, leaving local authorities to foot the bill.

The prison system itself can also suffer when its aim is profit and not the rehabilitation of prisoners. It costs less if you can put more people in each prison cell, even though experience has shown that this leads to victimisation and a rise in gang culture. Fewer prison guards means a lower wages bill, even if it puts the few remaining guards at greater risk. Problem cases are more and more frequently dealt with with extended periods of solitary confinement, which is known to worsen depression, antisocial feeling and violent tendencies.

This latter tactic is being used more and more frequently with young offenders, a group that even the most cynical would admit has the best chance of escaping from the vicious circle of crime and punishment. It has also been shown that teenagers suffer these bad reactions even after temporary isolation, and that it can trigger or worsen mental illness in them. But solitary confinement is the easiest way to deal with such problems and it is often used as a threat and as punishment, since being alone is what they dread the most.

We need to decide once and for all what we want from our prisons. When we convict someone of a crime and sentence them to imprisonment, are we simply saying we want them off the streets for six months, two years or even for life? Do we want someone who commits a crime to fear doing it again because prison is so terrifying? To some extent, perhaps we do. But surely, in this day and age, revenge, punishment, public protection and deterrence are not the only reasons for putting the guilty in prison. If we believe in people's capacity for change, we must commit to the rehabilitation that prisons can offer, and that is something that private prisons are unable to do.

1 What can we understand from the first paragraph?

A The US justice system is less likely today to jail people for minor offences.

B Record numbers of people are serving sentences in US prisons.

C Private prisons in the US are generally used for special types of prisoner.

D The US government intends to imprison a larger number of criminals.

2 Who are the 'customers' in the second paragraph?

A prisoners

B judges

C volunteers

D prison workers

3 Towns with private prisons have an interest in prison sentencing because

A many local residents work in the prisons.

B some citizens have family in jail.

C the prison authorities will help them to borrow money.

D they don't want to see more prisons built.

4 In the fourth paragraph, it is implied that

A public prisons don't use solitary confinement.

B prison officers in private prisons get lower wages.

C the best way to deal with violent offenders is to isolate them.

D private prisons are more dangerous and violent than public ones.

5 According to the writer, teenage offenders

A only become violent after long periods in solitary confinement.

B are more likely to be rehabilitated than other criminals.

C need time alone to think about their actions.

D usually suffer from serious mental illness.

6 What does the writer believe about the public prison system?

A Its sole purpose is to make sure prisoners never reoffend.

B Its programme must include some form of higher education.

C If privatised, it will not be able to perform its vital role.

D Its role is to punish offenders and offer revenge to victims.

Skills tip

With questions that ask you what the writer 'implies', what you can 'infer', what is 'suggested' or what can be 'understood' from a part of the text, don't search for the part of the text where one of the options is mentioned. In fact, if you find an exact match, it's a good clue that that option is NOT the correct answer. Try to think generally about the impression, feeling and meaning you got from the phrase, sentence, paragraph or entire text. Once you have a clear idea of it, look at the options and choose the one that is closest to what you were thinking.

Answer key

Unit 1

Improve your reading skills
1 B   2 A   3 A   4 B

Get started
The photo shows a relay race.
Students' own answers to remaining questions

Develop your vocabulary

1
1 lose
2 keep
3 defeat
4 hold
5 score

2
1 participants
2 teamwork
3 talents
4 group
5 championship
6 strategy
7 positions
8 tough
9 contact
10 helmets

Develop your reading skills

1
1 Rene Lucci, football, scored winning goal
2 Alan Lock, sailing, record holder
3 Don Clark, bowling, won top prize
4 Babe Ruth, baseball, scored 714 home runs
5 Ann Meyers, basketball, first high school student on US national team
6 Antonio Diez, water polo, won gold medal

2
1 4, 5
2 3
3 2, 4, 5, 6
4 2
5 6
6 5

3
1 group effort
2 exactly the same time
3 eight
4 six to eight
5 wooden
6 the catch
7 the release
8 muscle training

4
1 f   2 e   3 c   4 d   5 b   6 a

5
a disappointing loss
b thrilling overtime
c Stadium; national championship
d broken ankle
e wins big
f Training; to start

6
1 a   2 d

7
1 F   2 T   3 T   4 F   5 F   6 T

8

Player	Andy	Beth	Paul
Sport	basketball	cycling	polo
Practice days	weekdays	Mondays and Wednesdays	weekends
Practice length	an hour and a half	two hours	three hours (twice a week)
Likes	having energy throughout the day	practising whenever she likes	being with his horse
Dislikes	waking up early	some teammates don't meet every week	field not maintained well

9
information to be ticked: 2,4,5,7

10
2 primary school pupils
4 involves hitting another player
5 balls cannot be kicked nor can they be thrown at people's heads on purpose
7 if they catch your ball, you're out

Exam focus

1 c

2
1 A   2 B   3 A, B   4 B   5 B   6 B   7 A
8 B

3
1 on a beach or in a park
2 five players in each team
3 hitting the ball, serve the ball, throwing the ball, pass the ball
4 use a lot of energy, helps to be tall
5 pass the ball to one another
6 throwing the ball in one of the two baskets
7 server
8 placed at each end of the court, placed three metres high

Skills tip
a Yes, b Yes

Exam practice

1 B 'The main responsibility of a team captain, in my opinion, is to be optimistic that the team can win. So, before every game, I give a little pep talk to the team to motivate them.' and 'I'm there to tell them it's all right when they make a mistake, to give them praise for a job well done, to keep pushing them. That kind of support is essential if you want a chance of winning the league.'

2 D 'I've got several players who want to be strikers … A key part of my job is to make tough decisions about their roles'.

3 A 'I'm the only person on my team who can talk to the ref, and I always do that with the utmost politeness and respect, even if I strongly disagree with the call that's been made.'

4 C 'And the rules allow us to use our whole body in order to stop an opponent dead in their tracks. One issue I face as team captain is what to do about that.'

5 A 'Before the match, I … decide on the main strategy. … During the match, I need to constantly check players are sticking to the strategy we decided on'.

6 D 'Top footballers these days have the money and fame of royalty, and quite a few of the players at my level aspire to be like them. Basically, they all want to be stars!'

7 C 'I tell my team to generally play it safe, because what good are they to the rest of the team when they've been carried off on a stretcher?'

8 A 'During the match, I need to constantly check players are sticking to the strategy we decided on – but without too much micro-management, and being flexible depending on the situation.'

9 B 'So, before every game, I give a little pep talk to the team to motivate them.'

10 C 'I do my best to make sure … that the first-aid kit is well stocked!'

Unit 2

Improve your reading skills
1 B   2 B   3 B   4 A

Get started
Students' own answers

Develop your vocabulary

1 (Possible extra words in italics)
Accommodation: guest house, hotel, *5-star, motel, bed and breakfast*
Travelling: commute, luggage, *flight, journey, trip, timetable*
Problems: delays, jet lag, *travel sickness, stress, cancellations*

2
1 go in
2 go on
3 journey
4 travel
5 go with the

3
1 exotic
2 luxurious
3 foreign
4 local

Develop your reading skills

1
Suggested answers
1 The benefits of train/rail travel
2 The increased number of business trips taken by air / The past, present and future of air travel for business people
3 Commuting in the past
4 (Lesser-known) health concerns related to driving

2
Suggested answers
1 less pollution, fewer traffic jams, less stress, working/relaxing on the train, shorter journey times, saving money on petrol, etc
2 speed, comfort, globalisation, aircraft types, multinational businesses, accommodation, foreign cultures, ticket prices, statistics on the number of flights per year, etc
3 problems/advantages of commuting years ago, (lack of) comfort, safety/ dangers, journey time, etc
4 problems caused by sitting down for long periods, air pollution, loud music, stress, road rage, etc

3
Article 1: c, f, a
Article 2: b, e, d

4
Suggested answers
1 The advantages of business air travel
2 (Explanations for) bad behaviour among drivers / road rage
3 Illnesses that frequent business travellers suffer from
4 Examples of cultural differences (and their importance to business travellers)

5
1 c   2 d   3 f   4 a

6
Sentence a = Text 4 (before the sentence beginning, 'In the West… .')
Sentence b = Text 3 (after the sentence ending, 'careful about what you eat and drink.')
Sentence c = Text 1 (after the sentence ending, 'for just £69 return, if you book in advance.')
Sentence d = Text 2 (at the end of the text)

7
Suggested answers
Sentence a ('The business card', 'In Asia, these are usually … accepted with both hands.', 'In the West, we might casually accept… .')
Sentence b ('Stomach problems', 'be avoided, if you are careful about what you eat and drink.', 'recommend avoiding salads…may contain the bacteria', 'water that is not as pure as it should be.')
Sentence c ('flights from London to Glasgow for just £69', 'the price of petrol or a return train ticket would cost a great deal more.')
Sentence d ('every little event', 'can cause more anger and stress.', 'these all add up and cause an angry response.')

8
Suggested answers
1 Being late for an appointment or meeting
2 It may have been made with contaminated water.
3 Because in some cultures you are expected to remove your shoes in certain rooms.
4 £69
5 Up to half
6 The road space their car occupies

Exam focus

1
1 business people
2 positive and negative aspects

2
1 Paragraph 3
2 Paragraphs 4, 5 and 6
3 Paragraphs 5, 6 and 7
4 Paragraphs 1 and 2

3
Suggested answers
1 'People who take the train or drive long distances to meetings'
2 'less healthy food', 'sweets and snacks', 'fruit or a salad', 'Fitness Centre', 'healthier options on hotel menus', 'the healthiest meal', 'eat half a portion', 'walking as much as possible'

3 the opinions of Fiona Valentine and Daniel Long

4 'jetting off to a foreign country,' 'flying through different time zones can cause jet lag', 'links between flying and', 'on a long-haul flight' (Note that flying is also mentioned in Paragraph 3 but this is not the main topic of the paragraph.)

4

Suggested answers

Gap 1 b – The whole of the paragraph up to the gap is about the location and nearby amenities. It would be unusual to change the subject at this point, but guests at this hotel would want to know how accessible it is.

Gap 2 c – The sentences before and after the gap are about the hotel's facilities. It would be odd to introduce either of the other two options in the middle of this paragraph.

5

Suggested answers

Gap 1 Both the airport and the railway station are close to the hotel and can be reached by taxi or bus.

Gap 2 In addition, there is a conference room / a snack bar / 24-hour reception service / room service / etc.

Skills tip

a Yes, b Yes

6

1 F 2 T 3 T 4 T

Exam practice

1 C The preceding paragraph is clearly about the health risks involved with flying. This sentence concludes the section with its references to flying 'many times a year' and 'the risks'. After the gap, the writing moves away from flying as a means of transport.

2 G The sentence before the gap talks about the health issues associated with taking the train or driving. The missing sentence continues this idea with 'even a short daily commute' and the idea of raised blood pressure. After the gap, this is echoed in the reference to increased stress levels.

3 A The paragraph is about food. The sentence before the gap talks about eating while travelling and the missing sentence continues this idea with 'And when they reach their destination', followed by a further reference to food ('a big meal').

4 B The first sentence in the paragraph talks about food and exercise from the point of view of a fitness expert. The next sentence mentions loss of motivation to keep fit. The missing sentence refers to the problem people have with their fitness regime when they are 'away from home'. The sentence after the gap follows chronologically with 'Then, when they return' and the mention of getting back to their routine.

5 D The missing sentence refers to 'how many kilometres you can cover' at an airport. This follows the recommendation to walk 'as much as possible' while travelling.

6 F The missing sentence contains the idea of a place to stay with 'a bit more character'. This contrasts with the sentence before the gap, which mentions hotel chains being 'pretty much the same everywhere'. After the gap, we have examples of 'character' in 'a family-run guest house', as well as the idea of meeting 'local people'.

Unit 3

Improve your reading skills

1 A 2 B 3 B 4 A

Get started

Students' own answers

Develop your vocabulary

1

1 industry
2 media
3 fan
4 red-carpet
5 networking
6 judging

2

1 celebrity
2 eye
3 performance
4 costume
5 talented
6 audiences

3

1 c 2 d 3 a 4 b 5 e

Develop your reading skills

1

1 b 2 c 3 a 4 e 5 d

2

1 very loud
2 reserving a ticket
3 how many people watch a show
4 although
5 very

3

Suggested answers

1 in 2012
2 things young people have to face in their everyday lives
3 writing and directing
4 They have a negative image of young people.
5 positive
6 They worked with energy and enthusiasm.

4

1 tackle
2 issues
3 an awful lot
4 stage
5 threw themselves into it
6 set up

5

1 N 2 P 3 N 4 P 5 P

6

1 b 2 a 3 b 4 c 5 b

Exam focus

1

sentences to be ticked: 3, 4 and 6

Skills tip

a No, b Yes

2

1 b 2 d 3 e 4 a 5 c

3

Students' own answers

4

a

Exam practice

1 C The viewer says 'I discuss tactical voting strategies with other bloggers and we do our best to help our favourites win!' In this way, they can 'get the results they want'.

2 D A 'setback' is a problem or a change for the worse and the record producer mentions how CDs and DVDs 'knocked [the music industry] off its feet'. This section also talks about new social media being a 'threat'.

3 D The record producer says that the music industry was 'very slow to adapt to the new ways' and explains how they tried to 'stamp out' certain consumer activities. He/She goes on to say that they changed their tactics, using the word 'Then' to indicate what they did afterwards.

4 A The television executive talks about a 'golden age' which is a reference to the past and the question uses 'used to', which also refers to the past. He/She goes on to say that 'audiences today are far more sophisticated and no longer accept the idea of being spoon-fed their entertainment.' This is another way of saying that in the past viewers accepted 'whatever was offered to them.'

5 C The viewer comments on the presentation of entertainment acts. He/She says, 'I blog about whether the performance is any good, what the costumes are like …'.

6 B The actress says 'I have to be very careful about striking a balance between being a celebrity and a private person' and the question says that this person 'finds it difficult to separate their home life from their work'.

7 B The actress says 'the job … involves a great deal of self-promotion' and talks about 'keeping yourself in the public eye.' She also says that she uses Twitter to publicise her work. All of these are ways of 'maintaining her position in the industry'.

8 D The record producer talks about 'the unstoppable rise of new social networking sites as well as devices such as smartphones and tablet PCs, which give people easy access' and repeats this idea later in the text: 'the new ways in which people use technology to access entertainment.'

9 A The television executive says 'you have to come up with exciting new formats to keep the viewers tuned in', which means the same as 'fresh ideas to keep people interested'.

10 B The actress 'tries to involve [her] followers as much as possible' by publicising her work [on Twitter] so that she can keep her 'fan base up to date'. She explains that she wants her fans to 'feel that they're a part of the entertainment world, too.'

Unit 4

Improve your reading skills
1 A 2 B 3 B 4 A

Get started
Students' own answers

Develop your vocabulary

1
1 b 2 e 3 c 4 a 5 d

2
1 gain
2 apply
3 land
4 attend
5 send
6 offers

3
1 opportunity
2 employer
3 promotion
4 position
5 salary
6 CV

Develop your reading skills

1
1 c 2 a 3 b 4 b

2
1 c 2 d 3 a 4 b 5 e

3
1 a 2 d 3 c

4
1 education
2 spell, (simple) arithmetic
3 (modern) technology
4 tests

5
1 SD, MI
2 MI, SD
3 SD, MI
4 SD, MI

6
1 c 2 b 3 a 4 d

7
1 Tom McGregor
2 at 11am on Friday
3 £15,000
4 He was arrested.
5 He is a university graduate.
6 He had no job or money.

8
Suggested answer
A university graduate robbed a bank and nearly got away with £15,000.

Exam focus

1
1 beginning
2 after
3 Examples
4 Reasons
5 why the writer said something

Skills tip
a Yes, b No

2
Being the best candidate for the job is one thing. <u>That alone is not of much help, however, if you cannot persuade your potential employer that no-one else can do the job better than you.</u> This applies …

3
d

4
1 c 2 a 3 b

5
1 Part 6
2 Part 7
3 Part 6

Exam practice
1 B 'when many of my friends were enjoying what they termed their "final year of freedom", I was attending career fairs'.

2 D 'when I got home and found…, I made the pragmatic decision to widen my focus considerably.'

3 B 'Monday to Friday, I put in nine-to-five days (with a break for lunch) filling out online application forms, sending out CVs and following leads.'

4 C 'working as an unpaid intern' means the same as 'work for six months or a year without remittance'. The writer says the same thing in two different ways.

5 A 'Compare notes with university friends and you will find many are going through the same thing.'

6 D 'I could look back at my six months of unemployment as a waste of time, but I prefer to see it as a learning curve and a growth experience.'

Unit 5

Improve your reading skills
1 A 2 B 3 B 4 A

Get started
Students' own answers

Develop your vocabulary

1
1 sauté
2 roast
3 grill
4 steam
5 consume
6 boil

2

1 dietary
2 savoury
3 sprinkle
4 tasteless
5 dressing
6 spicy
7 greasy
8 vegan
9 tinned

Develop your reading skills

1
1 d 2 b 3 g 4 h 5 f 6 c 7 a 8 e

2
1 opinion article
2 advert
3 email
4 encyclopaedia
5 report
6 novel

3
1 F 2 T 3 T 4 T 5 T 6 F

4
a opinion article
b persuasive article
c news article
d story

5
1 c 2 a, b, c 3 b 4 d 5 c 6 d

6
1 c 2 c 3 d 4 a 5 b 6 a, b 7 none
8 none 9 b 10 b

7
1 a 2 b 3 a 4 a 5 b 6 a 7 a 8 a

8
1 e 2 d 3 a 4 f 5 g 6 b 7 c

9
c

Exam focus

1
a

2
c

3
1 B 2 C 3 A 4 B 5 D

Skills tip
a Yes, b No

4
b

Exam practice
1 C When the writer says, 'I wouldn't
   want to force my dietary beliefs upon
   them', he's saying he will eat what his
   friends prepare in order to be polite.

2 A The writer says, 'I started to consume
   less and less meat', which refers to a
   gradual process.
3 B Examples of vegetarian dishes in the
   text are 'broccoli…with rice and soy
   sauce', 'courgettes and aubergines in
   olive oil and basil', 'vegetable soup with
   pasta, creamy mushroom soup and
   spicy cabbage soup'.
4 B The writer says that there are too
   many vegetarians who 'believe that their
   way of eating is superior to any other.'
   This refers to them being arrogant.
5 D The text says 'for vegetarianism to
   take root in society', and then goes
   on to say 'for all to enjoy'. The second
   part is a key phrase because it means
   that vegetarianism would become
   'established' in this way.
6 D The writer expresses a summarising
   opinion in the middle paragraph,
   'What I discovered is that maintaining
   a vegetarian diet is not only healthy,
   delicious and inexpensive, it's also
   abundant in variety.' He goes on to
   make a suggestion at the end of the
   article. 'So, I propose that we, the
   vegetarians of the world … should
   become more relaxed about our meat-
   eating counterparts'.

Unit 6

Improve your reading skills
1 B 2 A 3 B 4 A

Get started
Students' own answers

Develop your vocabulary

1
1 b 2 e 3 a 4 c 5 d

2
1 set up
2 deforestation
3 smog
4 visibility
5 habitat
6 extinct
7 crops
8 mining
9 shortage
10 pesticides

Develop your reading skills

1
1 commitment
2 results
3 endangered species
4 fossil fuels
5 damage
6 pollution

2

1 a 2 b 3 a 4 c

3
1 and
2 As a result
3 Because of
4 However
5 In fact

4
1 However
2 he
3 This
4 but/although
5 but/although

5
1 No
2 Yes
3 No
4 No

6
Suggested answers
1 factories need to use cleaner forms of
   energy.
2 we have to do something about it
   quickly.
3 a lot of these chemicals are harmful to
   humans and animals.
4 thankfully most bird species are not in
   danger for now.
5 they don't do enough to protect the
   environment.
6 this has changed since the industrial
   revolution.

7
1 However/Nevertheless/Nonetheless
2 because
3 they
4 Also/Moreover/Furthermore
5 but
6 it
7 Despite

8
1 Yes
2 No (although 'This can only be
   achieved' fits grammatically, the ending
   'if people learn to respect their own
   environment.' doesn't logically connect
   with the idea of richer countries
   repaying poorer countries)
3 Yes

Exam focus

1
sentences to be ticked: 2,3,4,5,6

Skills tip
a No, b Yes

2
(suggested answer)
It's a photograph of the Earth from space.

3

b

4

sentences to be ticked: 1,2,3,5
(suggested answers for notes)

1 'clear image of it' and 'The photo' (see also the answer to 5)

2 'The photo' and 'It was taken'

3 'It was taken'

5 'image' and 'photo', 'tiny blue planet' and 'small and fragile'

5

c

Exam practice

1 C The first paragraph says 'There were two closely-related reasons'. The second paragraph starts with 'The first of these was'. The first gap has to introduce the second reason. After the gap, 'Manufacturing processes' relates to 'industry'.

2 F 'This was founded' refers to the Sierra Club.

3 A The Sierra Club was founded in the USA. After the gap, it talks about green organisations 'on both sides of the Atlantic', so we need a sentence in the gap that introduces the idea of either the UK or Europe.

4 G 'The city' refers back to 'London' and 'England's capital', 'its problems' refers back to 'air pollution' and 'tragedy' refers back to 'thousands of people had died'.

5 E 'this publication' refers back to 'a book…called *Silent Spring*'.

6 B The first two sentences of the final paragraph refer to the past. The sentences after the gap refer to now. The gap has to introduce the concept of now ('Today'). Also, 'no shortage of…groups' relates to 'But, even with thousands of green organisations'.

Unit 7

Improve your reading skills

1 B   2 A   3 B   4 A

Get started

Students' own answers

Develop your vocabulary

1

1 b   2 a   3 b   4 b   5 a

2

1 customs

2 values

3 roots

4 rituals

5 die out

3

1 d   2 a   3 e   4 c   5 b

Develop your reading skills

1

1 F   2 O   3 F

4 O   5 O   6 F

2

Suggested answers

1 whether opera is part of the country's traditional cultural life or not

2 The writer thinks that this is partly true.

3 Opera isn't open to people from all backgrounds or to younger people.

4 Yes. He or she says that there's a lot to be done to encourage greater participation.

5 the role of education and the role of the opera community itself in encouraging greater interest

6 They have not done enough to encourage people to enjoy opera.

3

sentences to be ticked: 1, 2, 3, 4, 6 and 9

4

Suggested answers

1 Personally, I think it's difficult to learn anything significant about a culture as a tourist.

2 I suppose the main cultural aspects which can express national identity are language, customs and cuisine.

3 I'm not sure that traditional cultures have much of a future in the modern world.

4 I would suggest that there's little point in preserving a culture if people have changed their way of life.

5

1

a G, b P

2

a P, b G

3

a G, b P

4

a P, b G

6

1 a   2 b

7

1 hugely

2 relaxed

3 perfectly

4 overweight

5 pleasant

8

1 b   2 b   3 b   4 a   5 b

9

1 b   2 e   3 a   4 c

Exam focus

1

1 a   2 b   3 a

2

sentences to be ticked: 1, 3 and 4

3

1 a   2 b   3 a   4 a

4

1 shameful (2b)

2 Most people agree (3a)

3 should (4a)

4 Unfortunately (1a)

Skills tip

a No, b No, c Yes

5

1 F   2 F   3 T   4 T

Exam practice

1 D The writer explains that people in their country use 'the skills which have been passed down to us from our parents' and grandparents' generations to create works of art.' This means the same as 'today's cultural activities are influenced by their ancestors'.

2 B The writer states that 'The downside of this, it seems to me, is that, as the country has become wealthier, many of our customs and even our values have changed.' This means the same as 'prosperity has affected traditions and beliefs'.

3 A The writer says 'Although we are one of the smaller north European countries, we have probably made a larger contribution to Europe's cultural traditions than our geographically larger neighbours' and the question asks for a comparison between 'the small size of their country' and 'its influence on the surrounding region'.

4 D The writer explains that the kites at the festival 'are believed to send a message to the gods asking for a good harvest.'

5 C The 'difficult past' mentioned in the question refers to 'a long and troubled history' and 'war and bloodshed' in the history of Armenia. And the 'cultural heritage' of the question refers to a phrase in the text which talks about how Armenia is 'rich in tradition'.

6 A The writer describes how the celebration of Juhannus is 'a mixture of the 1,000-year old Christian influence and the remains of old Finnish pagan traditions.' This is a combination of an ancient and a more modern religion.

7 A The event in question is the celebration of Juhannus. The writer explains that it was originally called 'Ukon juhla' and that at a later date it was named 'Juhannus' after John the Baptist.

8 B 'prestige' means honour or respect and this text explains how 'every musician on the islands fights for the honour of being named "Calypso Monarch"'.

9 B If a cultural event 'brings … people … together' it unites them. The writer says that 'two things unite everyone in this country' and explains that these factors are calypso music and the celebration of carnival.

10 C This text mentions 'Greek, Persian, Turkish and Arab influences' as having an effect on Armenia's 'cuisine, our folk dancing and music and our beautiful, bright traditional costumes'. The question also talks about 'all aspects of their culture'.

Unit 8

Improve your reading skills
1 B   2 B   3 A   4 A

Get started
Students' own answers

Develop your vocabulary

1
1 c   2 b   3 e   4 d   5 a   6 f

2
1 natural
2 public
3 bedside
4 mortality
5 Life
6 nurse

3
1 on
2 on
3 in
4 from
5 after
6 away

Develop your reading skills

1
1 beginners
2 pulled muscle
3 push
4 exercise

2
1 a   2 b   3 b   4 a

3
1 c   2 a   3 e   4 b   5 d

4
1 b   2 c   3 a   4 e   5 d

5
1 was entering
2 had/'d graduated
3 had not/hadn't prepared
4 Will/Can you take
5 was standing
6 had/'d had
7 jumped
8 has/'s been

6
1 previously
2 meanwhile
3 then
4 next
5 finally

7
1 b   2 a   3 d   4 e   5 c

8
1 b   2 c

9
1 b   2 a

10
1 d   2 a

Exam focus

1
sentences to be ticked: 1, 3, 4 and 6

Skills tip
a Yes, b No

2
b

3
1 a   2 b   3 c   4 a   5 c

4
1 F   2 F   3 T   4 T

Exam practice
1 B The paragraph talks about her education. The missing sentence lists the subjects which made up her education. In the sentence after the gap, 'The last of these ...' refers to 'mathematics'.

2 G The missing sentence tells us how she 'used her growing fame to great effect' by being instrumental in having a field hospital designed.

3 D The sentence before the gap is about Nightingale's book, *Notes on Nursing*. The first sentence of the paragraph which follows the gap continues talking about it. The missing sentence must therefore also be about her book: 'It is still in print'.

4 A This sentence follows naturally from the discussion of Nightingale's philosophy of patient care. The sentence that follows the gap shows how the graduates of the Nightingale School (mentioned in the missing sentence) did well and moved on to higher posts.

5 F The missing sentence gives an example of the 'massive improvement' (in soldiers' health in India) mentioned immediately before the gap.

6 E The sentence before the gap talks about how Nightingale was ill and bedridden. The missing sentence talks about 'being in great pain' and continuing to work from her sick bed.

Unit 9

Improve your reading skills
1 A   2 B   3 B   4 A

Get started
Students' own answers

Develop your vocabulary

1
1 d   2 f   3 g   4 a   5 h   6 j   7 c   8 e   9 b   10 i

2
1 up
2 up
3 off
4 to
5 out

Develop your reading skills

1
1 Celebrities are often surrounded by **symbols of wealth**. For example, if you visit their luxurious homes, you will probably see expensive sports cars parked outside.

2 When **actors achieve fame**, the signs of attaining success aren't hard to spot. For instance, when they go out in public, the paparazzi may follow them, or fans will approach them for autographs.

3 **A-list stars** are the most famous of actors, such as the ones who star in big Hollywood productions and the ones whose names always appear in the papers.

4 **Celebrities can find themselves in danger** due to their star status. One instance of this is when a stalker terrorises their everyday lives or when they receive threatening mail.

5 These simple **steps to success** are essential for any actor who wants to succeed in the world of acting. Firstly, an actor must <u>work hard at his or her craft</u>. Secondly, he or she <u>must actively seek auditions</u>. And thirdly, they need <u>just a bit of luck</u>.

6 They say that **nothing in life is free** and the **same applies to fame**. This can be seen in the way <u>celebrities pay thousands of pounds to look their best,</u> including the <u>fees they must pay to managers, lawyers and personal assistants.</u>

2

For example, For instance, such as, One instance of this, Firstly, Secondly, thirdly, This can be seen

3

1
assaulted a fan
numerous unpaid bills
uncontrolled aggressive behaviour

2
best-selling book
creative writing professor
literary genius

3
avoids the spotlight
lives in isolation
turns down award

4
massive crowd
packed audience
record ticket sales

4

Suggested answer
The first extract has no examples and the second extract is full of examples, including the specific venue and the names of those who attended the event.

5

Suggested answer
The second extract is more successful in describing the event because it gives specific examples which makes it more interesting for the reader.

6

1 h   2 g   3 c, f, i   4 d   5 e, a   6 b

7

1 alert the press to where they're going, celebrity wedding, wearing an outrageous outfit
2 the courtship, the wedding announcement, the enormous ring, the pre-nuptial agreement
3 Journalists make a big fuss; OR, the star gets their photo in all the magazines.
4 a bad reputation

8

1 b   2 a   3 c   4 e   5 d

9

a, c, d

10

Suggested answers
1 B   2 B   3 B   4 B   5 D   6 B or D
7 B   8 D

11

Suggested answers
sentences to be ticked: 2, 4, 5, 6 and 7

Exam focus

1 b

2

1 C   2 D   3 A   4 C

3

1 jogging through the neighbourhood, taking kids to school
2 shredding documents, burning things
3 overly-devoted fan, dangerous admirers

Skills tip

a No, b Yes

4

1 c   2 a   3 b

Exam practice

1 C Katie's one extraordinary feature was 'her ability to sing. That was the one superstar trait Katie would ever possess'. A 'superstar trait' is an extraordinary feature or quality.
2 A Katie's response, '"Oh, thanks, but you know, I'm just a small-town girl. I'm not the celebrity type," Katie replied with a shy smile', suggests she was reserved or shy.
3 C The tanned man's offer, '"We'll arrange everything for you. We'll pick you up, record some songs and if at any point you don't feel comfortable about anything, we'll call it quits, no worries"', was honest in nature and included an easy way out for Katie if she didn't like it. This indicates that Katie was under no obligation to the man.
4 D The text says that, 'Katie had an instant fan base, full of people who could relate to her…'. However, it also says that, 'media criticism was harsh, even unfair, regarding her appearance.' This means that the response was neither wholly negative nor wholly positive which is the same as 'a mixed response.'
5 B The text says that 'Katie's life had gone from a simple, quiet existence to a thrilling wild ride and finally to what she considered to be a terrible curse'. In the end, her life had become a nightmare.

6 D Immediately after the phrase '15 minutes of fame' is used in the text, the writer says 'So soon after becoming a star'. This refers to the short amount of time Katie spent as a celebrity.

Unit 10

Improve your reading skills
1 B   2 B   3 A   4 A

Get started
Students' own answers

Develop your vocabulary

1

1 take
2 make
3 go
4 course

2

1 qualification(s)
2 qualified
3 graduation
4 graduate
5 education
6 educated

3

1 to
2 for
3 option
4 market
5 level

Develop your reading skills

1

1 In addition
2 Because of this
3 However
4 At that time
5 It might be better to go
6 After

2

1 Because of this
2 In addition, Also, Furthermore
3 For instance
4 On the other hand, However
5 It might be better to go
6 At that time, Once you have gone, Before, After

3

1 b
2 both
3 a
4 both
5 b
6 a

4

a Vocational training, for example, is increasingly important.

b A little less than 1,000 years ago, universities began to be popular throughout Europe.

c The technological age has had a huge effect on education, with the rise of the internet making arguably the biggest difference.

d According to his autobiography, Charlton's college education was never about getting a job.

5

1 a 2 b and d 3 c

6

Suggested answers

1 'Although we tend to think', 'there is more to it than that', 'for example', 'We have long recognised', etc

2 (Text b) Past tenses, e.g. 'began', 'was/ were', 'continued'. Time references, e.g. 'A little less than 1,000 years ago', 'by the end of the 18th century'
(Text d) Past tenses, e.g. 'was', 'believed'. Time references, e.g. 'afterwards'

3 Narrative: Past tenses, e.g. 'took', 'has/ have had'. Time references, e.g. 'in the past'
Argumentative: 'To take just one example', 'This is in sharp contrast with'

7

1 feelings in a narrative – Text d – would fit equally well after sentence 1, 2, 3 or 4

2 examples – Text a – after sentence 2 or at the end of the paragraph

3 a contrasting idea – Text b – after sentence 2

4 events in a narrative – Text c – after sentence 2 or 3

8

Suggested answers

1 Topic sentence: There was a lot of pressure on James to go to university. / James was the only person who didn't want to go to university. / James strongly objected to going on to higher education, etc

2 Topic sentence: Study groups have a number of benefits. / There are a number of advantages to studying in a group. / Studying with other people is generally a good idea.

9

Paragraph 1 is about someone who went to Oxford University although he didn't want to.
Paragraph 2 is about the benefits (and one drawback) of study groups.

10

Suggested answers

Paragraph 1: narrative writing – 'First of all', 'Then, as James later found out', 'had convinced', 'Everyone seemed to be deciding', 'nobody was thinking', 'In the end', 'It was only later that'

Paragraph 2: argumentative (discursive) writing – 'First of all', 'Secondly', 'which can', 'Then', 'In addition', 'However'

11

Suggested answers

1 … there are times when it is good to share the opinions of others.

2 … it will give you a better chance of finding a good job.

3 … he decided to follow his dream and study poetry.

4 … have mobility problems or family obligations.

5 … still manage to study regularly, you should make the most of meeting new people.

6 … however, she felt as though she belonged there.

Exam focus

1

1 The text is about higher education and whether or not it is a good idea. The type of writing is argumentative/ discursive.

2

the benefits of having a higher education: Paragraphs 1, 2, 4, 7
the negative aspects of higher education: Paragraphs 3, 4, 5, 6
narrative writing (in the past tense): Paragraphs 2, 3
your choice of degree course: Paragraphs 2, 3, 4
money: Paragraph 6

Skills tip

a Yes, b No

2

Suggested answers

1 The most frequent difficulty encountered is one concerning academic work.
You would want to avoid failing exams or missing work.

2 The writer will probably write about good universities. It is possible that the writer might change direction here and talk about bad universities (introduced, for example, by 'However' or 'On the other hand'), but the sentence after the gap begins with 'However', so this is unlikely.

3 The writer will probably write about degrees which do not lead to a job. Archaeology graduates could be similar to graduates in another field. 'Unsuccessful' probably refers to finding a job.

4 The writer could add one further advantage of distance learning courses. Alternatively, there could be a 'change of direction' preceded, for example, by 'However' or 'On the other hand', where the writer adds a negative aspect. Clues to this could be found in the sentence after the gap.

3

1 c 2 a 3 d 4 b

4

All four points should be ticked.

Exam practice

1 C The words 'similarly successful' in the missing sentence refer back to 'close to 100% of graduates' in the main text. Also the phrase 'these subjects' in the missing sentence refers back to 'medicine, including dentistry' and 'these fields' in the preceding paragraph. Note too that after the gap, the writer changes the subject ('On the other hand,') to talk about degrees that are less likely to lead to a job.

2 F The phrase 'not in demand' in the missing sentence echoes 'less likely to find a job' in the text before the gap and previews the sentence after the gap. The missing sentence also introduces narrative writing with the present perfect ('have found out'), which is then continued in the simple past after the gap.

3 A The phrase 'less than ideal for you' echoes 'may not be your first choice' which appears in the text before the gap. 'However,' adds a condition to the sentence before the gap. The meaning of the missing sentence then links with the opening sentence of the paragraph after the gap, 'not everyone is suited to'.

4 D The missing sentence provides examples of the main idea which appears in the text before the gap, 'not everyone is suited to another three or four years of study. Some people are better off not continuing their education'. The sentences after the gap add more examples of this.

5 B The phrase 'financially secure' in the missing sentence echoes the subject of the paragraph, which is money. After the gap, the writer changes direction to talk about the benefits of higher education.

6 G The missing sentence provides an example of the 'benefits' mentioned before the gap. After the gap, there is a further example.

Unit 11

Improve your reading skills
1 B   2 A   3 B   4 B

Get started
Students' own answers

Develop your vocabulary

1
1 digital
2 programme
3 device
4 obsolete
5 system
6 revolutionary
7 operate

2
1 state-of-the-art
2 features
3 conventional
4 computerised
5 programmed
6 efficient
7 gadgets
8 models

Develop your reading skills

1
1 similar
2 like
3 comparison
4 compared
5 as
6 same

2
1 is similar to
2 looks (a bit) like
3 in comparison to
4 compared to
5 (not) as (good) as
6 in the same way as

3
1 simile
2 metaphor

4
1 S   2 S   3 S   4 M   5 M   6 S

5
1 F   2 T   3 F   4 T   5 T   6 F

6
1 like
2 only
3 also
4 to
5 more
6 as
7 better
8 most

7
1 more room (item 5), better than ever (item 7)
2 the most important (item 8)
3 it's your best friend
4 like a space-age gadget (item 1)
5 as many different appliances as (item 6)

8
1 F   2 T   3 T   4 F   5 T   6 T   7 T

9
1 in
2 to / with
3 much
4 the
5 like

10
Suggested answers
1 In the past you had to have lots of separate systems whereas today you only need one system.
2 You won't have as many cables with one system as you do with lots of systems.
3 a cinema and concert hall combined

Exam focus

1
questions 4 (compares … to) 7 (contrasts … to) and 10 (being similar to)

2
sentences to be ticked: 1, 4, 5 and 8

3
a 5 (Just as … so too), 8 (not as good … as)
b 1 (like a great, big, high-tech shopping centre)
c 4 (similar)

Skills tip
a Yes, b No, c Yes

4
1 B   2 A   3 A   4 B   5 A

Exam practice
1 B This text talks about 'so many different types of cookers and ovens – gas or electric, with or without a fan oven, a microwave, etc.' This means that there is a wide 'variety' available.
2 D Several references in the text justify this answer. 'Computers have begun to replace many other devices around the home, making them obsolete.' and 'Who needs all those gadgets of the past … when the computer can perform all their functions and more?'
3 A When talking about the washing machine, the writer says 'There is little doubt that the housewives of the past would have been delighted to use a modern washing machine'.
4 A In this text the writer describes a mangle as being 'a bit like a steam roller that is used to flatten the tarmac on highways!' which is a machine 'used for road maintenance'.
5 C In this text, the writer talks about how in the past you needed 'the muscles of a weightlifter to get your carpets clean'. This means that a person required 'a great deal of physical strength'.
6 D There are a number of references to the organisation of 'the most up-to-date homes'. In particular, 'Computers are increasingly used for entertainment and communication, for shopping and work and as a way of controlling other systems and devices in the home.' and 'State-of-the-art homes now use computer technology to run almost every aspect of domestic life'.
7 A The writer says 'Not only is the washing machine highly efficient and easy to use, it also saves on water, so it is more environmentally friendly than washing by hand.'
8 B In the past people had to 'use wood or coal to light a stove or cooking range and heat it for hours before it could even be used.' This is synonymous with 'an appliance from the past that took a long time to prepare'.
9 D In this text, the writer states that 'just as it has affected today's domestic technology, so too will it affect the domestic appliances of the future.' He or she is making 'a prediction' about the use of technology in the future.
10 C The writer compares the vacuum cleaner to 'a … housemaid' which is the same as 'a servant' mentioned in the question.

Unit 12

Improve your reading skills
1 A   2 B   3 A   4 B

Get started
Students' own answers

Develop your vocabulary

1
1 d   2 b   3 f   4 e   5 c   6 a

2
1 finds
2 commit
3 charge
4 convict
5 sentence

3
1 jury
2 lawyer's
3 bribery
4 bars
5 sentence
6 imprisonment

Develop your reading skills

1
1 a   2 b   3 a   4 a   5 b

2
1 c   2 a   3 e   4 b   5 d

3
Sentences to be ticked: 1, 3 and 5

4
1 sarcastic
2 angry
3 humorous
4 regretful

5
1 a   2 a   3 a   4 b

6
1a E, b I
2a I, b E
3a E, b I

7
1 c   2 b   3 a

8
1 Before I got here, it was fear of the unknown as much as anything else.
2 Then I'll be out, ready to get a job and look after you for a change.
3 I'm on the top one, and he's on the bottom.

9
Suggested answers
1 It's Mark's first time in prison.
2 Mark doesn't like it in prison.
3 Mark's mother was very upset in court.
4 Mark doesn't intend to commit crimes anymore.
5 Mark's mother is from Ireland.

Exam focus

1
sentences to be ticked: 1, 3 and 4

Skills tip
a No, b Yes

2
d

3
1 b   2 c   3 a

4
1 a   2 a

Exam practice
1 A In the first paragraph, it says the prison population has fallen slightly and that this is 'partly from a general recognition on the part of state and federal government that putting petty criminals behind bars was the least effective way to deal with crime.'
2 A After the first mention of 'customers' in the second paragraph, the text goes on to say 'What is unusual about them, though, is that their customers don't really want to use their services'. A person who 'uses' the prison service must be a prisoner. The text immediately after this sentence also refers to 'the criminal'.
3 A In the second part of paragraph 3 the text says 'There are also whole towns that depend on their prisons for employment'. This means the same as the question, i.e. that 'many local residents work in the prisons.'
4 D The paragraph begins by saying that private prisons are interested in making a profit and not in helping prisoners. It goes on to list all the ways in which this can be proved – 'more people in each prison cell', 'Fewer prison guards', 'extended periods of solitary confinement'. The writer also relates these phenomena to 'victimisation and a rise in gang culture', 'remaining guards at greater risk' and 'worsen depression, antisocial feeling and violent tendencies'. All of this equates to private prisons being 'more dangerous and violent than public ones.'
5 B In the fifth paragraph the writer says that young offenders have 'the best chance of escaping from the vicious circle of crime and punishment' which means that young people are more likely to become rehabilitated and to stop offending than other groups within the prison population.
6 C At the end of the final paragraph, the writer says 'we must commit to the rehabilitation that prisons can offer, and that is something that private prisons are unable to do.' In other words, if all prisons are privatised, the public prison system 'will not be able to perform its vital role' (that of rehabilitation).